160 Letters that Get Results

Ajay Patel

which?

Which? Books are commissioned and researched by
Consumers' Association and published by
Which? Ltd, 2 Marylebone Road,
London NW1 4DF
Email address: books@which.co.uk

First edition (published as *120 Letters that Get Results*) October 1991
Reprinted January and July 1992
Revised edition September 1992
Reprinted July 1993
Revised edition May 1995
Revised edition June 1996
150 Letters that Get Results first published March 1997
Revised edition April 1998
Reprinted January 1999
Revised edition May 2000
160 Letters that Get Results first published February 2003
This edition May 2005

British Library Cataloguing in Publication Data
A catalogue record for this book is available from the British Library

ISBN 1 84490 011 8

Help at hand

If you have ever been faced with the sort of problems described in this
book, you'll be glad to know that Which? has a service, open to all, which
allows you to consult some of the UK's top consumer lawyers by telephone at any time Monday–Friday (9am–5pm). For details of how to
subscribe to Which? Legal Service, either write to Which?, Gascoyne Way,
Hertford X, SG14 1LH, telephone free on (0800) 252100 or visit
www.which.co.uk. Information about other Which? books can be obtained
from Which? Books, PO Box 44, Hertford SG14 1SH.

Original cover design by Sarah Harmer
Cover photo by Digital Vision/getty images

Typeset by Saxon Graphics Ltd, Derby
Printed and bound by Creative Print and Design, Wales

Contents

★An asterisk next to the name of an organisation in the text indicates that the address can be found in this section

How to use this book

160 Letters that Get Results shows you how to make a written complaint (by letter or email) in the most effective way, using a standard format which you can adapt to suit your own problem and which employs the most appropriate phrasing and legal terminology.

To get the most out of this book, read the Introduction carefully before you write. It gives a basic summary of consumer rights and explains the key pieces of legislation.

The Introduction also takes you through the practical sequence of making a complaint, from the initial notification to the last resort, going to court. It is essential to bear in mind the advice it gives on managing your complaint – keeping records of telephone conversations and copies of all correspondence, for example – and on the elements of an effective letter, such as citing relevant legislation, using correct legal vocabulary and setting deadlines. All are components of a successful campaign to achieve what you want.

Once you have read the Introduction, consult the relevant chapter for your problem. If, for example, you are in dispute with a shop over a defective hair-dryer, turn to Chapter 1: Buying goods, and then read the text preceding the standard letters. This gives further advice regarding your rights and how to pursue them. Once you have digested this information, use the appropriate standard letter to address your problem.

Each letter has a title explaining to whom you should send it. Further, each one has been constructed to allow you to insert specific information where relevant – instructions to do this are given in square brackets throughout. It is important to remember that you are communicating in written form a fact that is often a visual one, so aim for clarity – say something like 'the on-off switch became loose, and the hair-dryer emitted blue sparks and a burning smell'.

The next paragraph generally sets out the legal basis of your claim and the obligations you are owed, again with elements for you to complete. The final paragraph sets a date for a response. The whole letter shows that you intend to pursue the matter, and its tone, though formal and polite, is firm.

Should the recipient deny your claim, you should then use the subsequent letter and, can, if necessary, carry out your threat of instigating court action by following the guidelines in Chapter 17: Going to court.

All the letters in this book can be adapted to individual cases as required, and you will be advised of those circumstances in which it is appropriate to make 'time of the essence' or to head your correspondence 'without prejudice'. You will also be warned of situations in which it is essential to seek professional legal advice.

Many of the chapters give updated information on the proposed changes in legislation at the time of going to press. However, you can keep up to date on most consumer issues by contacting your local advice centre, Citizens Advice Bureau or Trading Standards Department, or by getting in touch with Which?*.

Some websites also provide excellent access to further information and advice to consumers. The Consumer Direct Gateway (*www.consumerdirect.gov.uk*) provides an overview of those issues that cause most concern to consumers and a way in to other websites with consumer information and advice run by government departments, consumer organisations and others including the umbrella bodies for local Trading Standards Departments. Community Legal Service Direct (*www.clsdirect.org.uk*) provides useful access to consumer help and advice online. Another helpful site is the one run by the Advice Services Alliance, whose members include Citizens Advice, Shelter and Advice UK. It can be found at *www.advicenow.org.uk*.

The Office of Fair Trading (OFT)* also provides excellent leaflets advising on a wide range of consumer problems.

Throughout this book, for 'he' read 'he or she'.

Introduction

What can you do if your new car goes badly wrong but the garage refuses to take it back? What should you do if the work you have just had done in your kitchen is not up to standard, or you are in dispute with an electricity company because you think your bill is too high? Perhaps your holiday did not live up to the glowing description in the tour operator's brochure or the computer accessories you bought on the Internet did not work. How do you go about obtaining satisfaction? When something goes wrong with the goods or services you have bought, it does not have to be time-consuming and expensive to get matters put right.

To make a successful complaint, it helps if you know your legal rights as a consumer. You also need to know how to complain effectively: approaching the right person and setting out your claim in the right way, using appropriate language and stating your case clearly will increase your prospects of success and redress. This introduction summarises the law governing consumer problems and provides detailed advice on putting together a fruitful letter of complaint. From time to time you may need to use legal language, which has precise meaning and may imply more than is immediately obvious to a lay person – see the Glossary at the back of the book for explanations of the key words and phrases.

Your rights – a summary

Before making a complaint, make sure you know exactly what you want to achieve. Do you want money – a refund or compensation? Do you simply want an apology from the person or organisation to whom you are complaining? Whatever it is you are seeking should be made clear from the outset. You should also be certain of your legal rights. When something goes wrong with the goods you have bought, or services are not up to scratch, knowing your rights as a consumer puts you in a stronger position to resolve the problem to your advantage. The basics of consumer law are explained below, while subsequent chapters provide further details of your rights in specific circumstances.

Buying goods

Every time you buy goods from a shop, street market, mail-order company or the Internet, or from any other kind of supplier, you enter into a contract with the seller. A contract is an agreement defined by law, and it gives you certain legal rights. Under the Sale of Goods Act 1979 as amended by the Sale and Supply of Goods Act 1994 the goods must:

- **fit the description** used in any advertisement, label, packaging and so on relating to them – the year or make, type, colour, size or materials used, for example, must all be accurately described
- **be of satisfactory quality** – the goods should work properly, have no major or minor defects, be safe, and, if new, look new and be in good condition
- **be fit for their purpose** – if you made it clear to the retailer when choosing goods that you needed them for a specific purpose, they must fulfil those requirements.

If goods you have bought do not meet these requirements, the retailer is under a legal obligation to sort out your problem. You may be able to reject the goods and get your money back. See pages 24–25 for more details on your rights when buying goods.

Some special cases

Delivery times
If it is clear that the goods you have ordered are required by a specific date, such as Christmas cards, and they do not arrive in time, you are entitled to cancel your order and to get your money back. And if you have to pay more to buy the goods else-where, you can demand the difference in price from the initial supplier.

If no delivery date is fixed, the supplier is under a legal obliga-tion to send the goods within a reasonable time. If you need to receive the goods by a specific date, let the supplier know in writing that 'time is of the essence' and set a date for delivery. By doing so, you make the delivery date an important term of the legally binding contract between you.

Mail order

You may have extra protection under the codes of practice governing mail-order purchases, so check with the relevant trade associations (see Addresses at the back of this book). If you pay when you order in response to an advertisement which carries the appropriate logo and which appears in a national newspaper that is a member of the Mail Order Protection Scheme (MOPS)*, and the company to which you sent your order goes into liquidation, you can reclaim your money through that scheme. But you cannot do so if the advertiser does not have the MOPS 'seal of approval'.

Credit

Whether you pay for faulty goods or services in cash or by credit card, your claim for redress is against the seller. But paying by credit card, such as MasterCard or Visa, gives you the added protection of the Consumer Credit Act 1974, provided the goods cost over £100. If you pay by this means, then along with the seller, the credit-card company is also liable for the faulty goods or services. This is useful if, for example, the retailer goes bust (see page 161).

If you buy on credit through a hire purchase agreement, credit sale or conditional sale, the finance company, *not* the seller, is responsible to you for the quality of the goods. You also have more time in which to reject goods on hire purchase (see page 162).

Private purchases

When you buy goods from a private individual, the only responsibilities on the seller are that he must own the goods and that the goods must correspond with any description you have been given. So if you buy a car from a private advertisement in a newspaper, you cannot complain if it breaks down after a week unless it was described, for example, as being in perfect working order.

Sales

If you buy goods at reduced prices in a sale, you still retain all your rights under the Sale of Goods Act. However, if you are buying goods described as 'seconds', be certain to find out before you buy them exactly what defect makes them not of first quality. You cannot complain later about that defect, but if the goods develop a different fault you can complain about that fault to the retailer. Notices in shops to the effect that no refunds are made on sale goods have no basis in law – if the goods are faulty, you are entitled to a refund. Such notices are unlawful unless they say 'This does not affect your statutory rights', and should be reported to your local Trading Standards Department.

Services

When you ask someone to carry out a service for you, such as building work, plumbing or dry-cleaning, you enter a legally binding contract which gives you basic legal rights. As well as the right to receive the service that is defined in the terms of the contract (types of materials that will be used, dates by which the work will be done, and so on), you also have legal rights implied into the contract. The Supply of Goods and Services Act 1982 (common law in Scotland) states that the work covered by the contract must be carried out with reasonable skill and care. It also says that if the contract does not specify precise dates or prices, the work must be carried out within a reasonable time and for a reasonable price. Again, 'reasonable' is not always clearly defined, but usually depends upon whether or not another supplier would have done the same as the firm you are claiming against.

If something goes wrong as the result of a service – your new plaster starts to crack, or the roof which you had mended still leaks – first ask the contractor to put the defects right. If the contractor will not do so, you are legally entitled to employ another to rectify the problem – and then claim the cost from the first contractor.

Other important consumer legislation

Other legislation conferring individual consumer rights includes:

Arbitration Act 1996, and, in Scotland, the Consumer Arbitration Agreements Act 1984

If the disputed sum is under £5,000 in England and Wales (or £750 in Scotland), consumers are not legally bound by clauses in contracts which state that any dispute must be referred to arbitration; they have the choice of court *or* arbitration.

Consumer Credit Act 1974

This regulates credit agreements and gives purchasers a number of rights: advertisements for credit schemes must show true rates of interest without hidden extras; purchasers have certain rights to pay off the debt before the time stipulated in the agreement; purchasers who sign a credit agreement at home have a cooling-off period during which they may change their mind and cancel the agreement. The Act is currently being reviewed.

Consumer Protection Act 1987, and, in Northern Ireland, the (N.I.) Order 1987

This states that: (1) manufacturers are strictly liable if the products they make are defective and cause personal injury, or damage to your property over £275; (2) all goods must comply with a general safety requirement; and (3) bogus bargain offers are controlled.

Consumer Protection (Cancellation of Contracts Concluded Away from Business Premises) Regulations 1987

This gives purchasers a seven-day cooling-off period during which they have the right to cancel certain contracts made during an unrequested visit by a salesperson to their home even when they are not buying on credit. These rules have been extended to include situations when you receive an unannounced visit and agree to the salesperson coming back another time. If the visit is classed as 'unsolicited' (i.e. uninvited) the salesperson commits a criminal offence if he fails to tell you about your right to cancel and can be fined up to £2,500 by the Trading Standards Department.

Contracts (Rights of Third Parties) Act 1999

The Act alters the rule of privity of contract, which meant that you could take an action to enforce a contract only if you were a party to it, and brings the law in England and Wales into line with Scotland. Before this Act, if you bought a gift for someone else and it turned out to be faulty, the recipient of the gift would, strictly speaking, not have any recourse against the shop because he was not a party to the contract. The Act now allows the recipient to take action provided that at the time of making the contract the purchaser specifically agrees with the retailer that the third party is to have the benefit and that the Act applies. This should be done in writing.

Disability Discrimination Act 1995

Since October 1999, service providers, including shops, hotels and restaurants, have had to make 'reasonable adjustments' to ensure access for disabled people to their services, for example providing those who are hard of hearing with written information, or allowing guide dogs on to premises. From October 2004, service providers have had to make 'reasonable adjustments' to the physical features of their premises to overcome barriers to access.

Enterprise Act 2002

The Act gives the Office of Fair Trading (OFT)★ substantial powers to act against unfair business practices. It also gives other bodies like Trading Standards and Which? the legal right to stop traders conducting their business in breach of legislation. The Act also gives such bodies the power to make a super-complaint when an industry appears to be harming the interests of consumers.

Human Rights Act 1998

The Human Rights Act is an important, wide-ranging law which came into effect in 2000. It affects almost every part of our lives. The Act does not spell out things you must or must not do – it's more like a set of principles covering an individual's relationships with public bodies, such as the police, local councils and government agencies. The Act normally cannot be used against a private company.

Occupiers' Liability Act 1957

This gives people the right to claim compensation if they are injured due to negligence while visiting someone's premises.

Misrepresentation Act 1967, and, in Northern Ireland, the Misrepresentation Act (N.I.) 1967

If consumers enter an agreement on the basis of a statement purporting to be a fact but which turns out to be untrue, they have the right to cancel the deal and get their money back if they act quickly, or to compensation. The Act does not apply to Scotland. However, Scottish law is broadly similar.

Sale and Supply of Goods Act 1994
This law updates the Sale of Goods Act 1979. It replaces the outdated phrase 'merchantable quality' with 'satisfactory quality' and generally gives consumers improved rights.

Supply of Goods (Implied Terms) Act 1973
This defines purchasers' rights when buying on hire purchase: the goods must correspond to their description, be of satisfactory quality and reasonably fit for their purpose.

Unfair Contract Terms Act 1977
The small print in contracts for the sale of goods cannot take away purchasers' rights under the Sale and Supply of Goods Act. These and other notices or conditions in contracts which exclude or restrict liability for financial loss or damage to property must be fair and reasonable. If they are not, they will be invalid under the Act and will not affect a claim.

Sale and Supply of Goods to Consumers Regulations 2002
This law improves consumers' rights when they buy faulty goods. If a fault appears in goods in the first six months it is up to the seller to prove that the goods were not faulty at the time of sale. If he cannot, it will be assumed that the goods were faulty. The Regulations also enable the buyer to enforce very specific rights including repair, replacement or refund.

Unfair Terms in Consumer Contracts Regulations 1999
The Unfair Terms in Consumer Contracts Regulations 1999 set out the law on unfair contract terms in standard form contracts. The Regulations cover consumer contracts with businesses made after 1 July 1995. They add to and do not replace existing protection for consumers, particularly that provided by the Unfair Contract Terms Act 1977. The aim of the Regulations is to stop companies using unfair small print. The OFT and other qualifying bodies including Which?★, the Financial Services Authority (FSA)★, the Office of Gas and Electricity Markets (OFGEM)★, the Office of Water Services (OFWAT)★, the Office of Communications (OFCOM)★, the Office of Rail Regulation (ORR)★, the Information Commissioner★ and local Trading

Standards Departments are now able to act against unfair consumer contracts.

Unsolicited Goods and Services Act 1971

This gives recipients of unrequested and unwanted goods the right to get rid of them without paying for them.

Criminal laws

Certain criminal laws also affect consumers. Although they do not entitle consumers to get compensation directly, reporting a criminal offence will provide support for the complaint. The most relevant laws are the following.

Consumer Protection Act 1987

This stipulates that only safe goods should be put on sale and prohibits misleading price indications.

Food Safety Act 1990

This covers food standards and hygiene wherever food is manufactured, prepared or sold, as well as other aspects of food and drink.

Trade Descriptions Act 1968

This makes it a criminal offence for traders to make false statements about the goods they sell.

How to make an effective complaint

If you discover a defect in goods soon after purchase, act quickly. Insist on speaking to the manager of the establishment where you bought them or to someone else in authority who can make a decision about the problem. Addressing your complaint to the right person is more likely to resolve the problem to your satisfaction.

Keep a record of any verbal complaint

You may of course complain in person initially, but if you complain by telephone make sure you have a pen and some paper to hand so that you can keep a record of the conversation. In either case, always ascertain the name and position of the person to whom you are speaking. Write these down, together with the date and details of your conversation. Your records of such conversations will be important if you have to take your claim further.

Send a letter of complaint

Unless your problem is resolved immediately, follow up your verbal complaint by letter or email. Address it to the person immediately responsible for sorting out the problem, having ascertained his name and position. By sending your letter to a named individual you reduce the chance of its being passed round the organisation and perhaps being ignored or lost. The letter should ideally be typed. If this is not possible, write as neatly as possible to ensure legibility. Always date letters. It also makes sense, especially when dealing with large organisations like insurance companies and tour operators, to give the letter a heading such as the name and number of your insurance policy, your holiday booking reference and so on. Use this heading, and any reference given to you by the organisation, every time you write.

When – in keeping with our advice – you ascertain the name of the person to whom to address your complaint, use 'Yours sincerely' in the letters in this book. In instances where you do not know the addressee's name, use 'Yours faithfully'.

Keep to the point

Keep your letter brief, with short paragraphs setting out the details of your problem. Stick to the facts, making sure they are correct (model number of the goods, date of purchase, the nature of the defect, etc.). Avoid repetition. Do not make personal remarks in your letter, however justified they may seem to be. Keep your letter polite and never lose your temper – this will not help your claim and may make it more difficult to settle the problem. But you should be firm.

State the legal basis of your claim

Let the person to whom you are complaining know the legal basis of your claim, and, if possible, include brief details of the relevant piece of law covering your case. Mentioning, for example, the Sale of Goods Act 1979 if you are complaining about faulty goods or the Supply of Goods and Services Act 1982 in respect of inadequate services, for example, shows that you are aware of your rights and mean business.

State what redress you are seeking

Be clear about what you want to achieve and specify what you want from the other party, whether it is your money refunded, a repair or a replacement of the defective item. If you want financial compensation, spell out why and state the exact sum that you expect to receive. Bear in mind that while you have legal rights to redress you are also under a legal obligation to keep your claim as small as is reasonably possible.

Set a deadline

Set a deadline by when you want a response from the other party. Be reasonable and do not give too short a period of time for the individual or organisation to respond appropriately. If it is a simple matter of giving you a refund, 14 days is a reasonable time in which to expect your letter to be answered and the cheque sent. If you want repairs done to faulty building work, such as a leaky new roof, a longer deadline for a response would be appropriate, because the builder may be committed to carrying out other jobs in the near future and may need time to make suitable arrangements to put your problem right.

Stick to deadlines

You should keep to the time limits that you have imposed on the other party. That way your claim will be taken more seriously by the person or organisation to whom you are complaining.

You should also watch out for any time limits set out in specific complaints procedures. For example, insurance claims, and claims for compensation for luggage lost or damaged by airlines, have to be made within specific time limits. If you leave it too late to complain, you may lose your right to compensation.

Use recorded delivery

Send important letters by recorded delivery – you get a record of posting and a signature is obtained by the postman on delivery. This will prevent the other party from claiming not to have received your letter. If sending emails, keep the record showing delivery.

Get evidence

Once you have decided to write, collect any evidence you can to support your claim: invoices, receipts, holiday brochures and confirmation invoices (if you are complaining about a holiday), advertisements, estimates, bills, the names and addresses of witnesses, car registration numbers (if you are making an insurance claim) and so on. Photographs of any damage that has been caused – from a leaky roof or cracked kettle – or, for example, of dirty holiday accommodation, can also help your case. If appropriate, obtain written evidence from an independent technical expert in the trade concerned and written confirmation from witnesses of what they saw, heard and experienced. If your complaint is disputed, you will have to prove your case, and evidence in support of your claim, particularly expert evidence, may well tip the balance of the argument in your favour.

Keep copies of relevant documents

Do not send original documents with your letters. Send photocopies and keep the originals in a safe place in case you need to produce them at a later date. Take care not to add further damage to the items which are the object of your complaint. When you discover that goods are faulty, stop using them immediately, particularly if you want to get rid of them and claim a refund.

Always keep a copy of your letters – you may need to refer to them later if you are unable to settle your dispute easily and have to take further action such as using an arbitration scheme, referring the matter to an ombudsman or, in the last resort, taking the case to court.

Be persistent

If you fail to get what you want at your first attempt, be persistent: write another letter of complaint setting out your dissatisfaction. Your first letter of complaint may not be enough to get your problem resolved. So be firm and show that you mean business – that way you are more likely to get redress. Do not fall prey to attempts to fob you off with less than you are entitled to, such as the following.

'We do not guarantee products' This has no basis in law. Your rights as a consumer apply whether you have a written guarantee or not.

'It is not our problem. Try the manufacturer' This is not true. Your contract is with the trader who supplied the goods or services and that party is legally obliged to put things right.

'We do not give refunds' This statement is not supported by consumer legislation. If the goods you have bought are not as described, of satisfactory quality, or fit for their purpose, you are entitled to a refund if you act quickly enough. Notices saying 'No refunds given' are against the law. Report shops displaying them to your local Trading Standards Department.

'You are too late. You should have complained within 30 days' Do not accept time limits of this sort. Whether you are complaining about goods or services, even if it is too late to get a full refund (i.e. the 'reasonable' period of time has elapsed), your rights to compensation last for six years (five years in Scotland).

'You caused the problem, not us' You should not be deterred by this kind of tactic. If, for example, the floor you have just had laid in your bathroom starts to warp because of contact with water, do not be put off claiming. Bathroom floors should withstand water and if the flooring does not do so it is not fit for its purpose, so you are entitled to claim. If the problem is not as clear-cut as this, you may need an independent test on the item.

'We cannot do anything without a receipt' Having a receipt is not a legal requirement for obtaining redress. If the trader asks for proof of purchase, a receipt is useful. A credit-card voucher, for example, would be legally acceptable.

'No refunds on sale items' Goods bought in a sale are still covered by consumer legislation. If you buy seconds, you cannot expect them to be perfect, but they must still be of satisfactory quality (i.e. free from hidden defects) and as described. But you are not entitled to compensation for any defects which were pointed out to you at point of purchase or which you should have spotted before buying.

Follow the right complaints procedure

Where there is one, you should always adhere to the proper complaints procedure established for your particular problem. Missing out a step in the procedure by complaining to someone inappropriately senior in the organisation or to the wrong body or watchdog may lead to your letters being ignored or redirected, which will cause delay. You may also cause unnecessary antagonism, which may damage your chances of success.

Suppliers of gas and electricity and professions like the law and medicine have their own mechanisms for dealing with complaints. Turn to the relevant chapters later in the book for detailed explanations of these procedures.

Be reasonable when considering an offer

It pays to be reasonable and to be prepared to come to an agreement if you receive a fair offer, even if it is not exactly what you wanted at the outset.

However, you should bear in mind that accepting an offer of compensation normally means that you cannot ask for more later. If you are uncertain about accepting an offer, take legal advice.

To avoid committing yourself by mistake when negotiating figures for a compromise settlement, write 'Without prejudice' at the top of that part of your correspondence. That way those letters cannot be held against you and cannot be revealed if you finally have to go to court to pursue your claim. But do not write 'Without prejudice' on the rest of your letters – those in which you set out and pursue the main basis of your claim, for instance.

Get expert advice

If you need help in pursuing your claim, contact your local Citizens Advice Bureau, consumer advice centre, law centre or, particularly if you have been injured, a solicitor. (Some solicitors offer free advice under the Accident Line★ service.)

Take formal action

If all else fails, the following courses of action may be open to you.

Court The final stage before initiating court action is to send a 'letter before action', giving notice to the other party that unless you receive redress within a specified period (usually seven days) the matter will be taken to court (see pages 269–70). The small claims track in the county court (small claims procedure in the sheriff court in Scotland) is a cheap and informal way of dealing with claims up to £5,000 (£2,000 in Northern Ireland, £750 in Scotland). Personal injury claims are limited to £1,000 in England; see page 299 for claims in Scotland. For information on going to court, see Chapter 17.

Alternative Dispute Resolution The courts are now encouraging both parties to use Alternative Dispute Resolution (ADR) to resolve the claim by conciliation or mediation, for example. When you have issued a claim form and the other party has entered a defence you will have to fill in an allocation questionnaire. This will ask if the parties want a one month's stay (which means putting the case on hold) to see whether the matter can be resolved through ADR. You cannot be forced to use ADR, but you should give it careful consideration – even before court action is started. Once the matter is resolved, the court will look at whether the parties acted reasonably as well as the eventual outcome when deciding what costs to award. If the court considers that you unreasonably failed to consider ADR you may find that you will not recover all the costs you are entitled to, even if you win your case.

Arbitration Various trade and professional bodies offer their own low-cost arbitration schemes. The Chartered Institute of Arbitrators* (Arbiters in Scotland) will give an independent decision on your dispute if both you and the other party agree to it. However, if you lose you may have to pay the arbitrator's costs – which can be expensive. If there is no clear loser, you will have to pay a share of the costs, which again could be considerable.

Ombudsmen These are traditionally seen as a means of resolving disputes between individuals and public- or private-sector bodies. Examples of public-sector ombudsmen are the Parliamentary Commissioner and the Local Government Ombudsmen. The Financial Ombudsman Service★ covers many financial services, such as insurance, building societies and banking.

Usually you must take up your claim with the company's head office first. After that, you can apply to the relevant Ombudsman to investigate a complaint. The service is free, and if you are not happy with the final decision you can still pursue your claim in the courts.

Chapter 1

Buying goods

The word 'goods' covers almost everything apart from land and houses – from pets to cars and computer software. Every time you buy goods from a shop, mail-order company, garage or any kind of retailer, you enter into a contract with the seller. This contract gives you certain rights that are backed by the Sale of Goods Act 1979 as amended by the Sale and Supply of Goods Act 1994. These rights have been further strengthened by the Sale and Supply of Goods to Consumers Regulations 2002, which apply to purchases made after 31 March 2003.

Your rights

The law says that you are entitled to goods of satisfactory quality. In other words, the goods should work properly, be free from minor defects, be safe and, if new, look new and be in good condition. And depending on what it is you are buying, the goods should also last a reasonable amount of time.

If you tell a retailer that you require goods for a specific purpose, then as well as being fit for their more general purpose, the goods should also be fit for that specific purpose. This obligation applies only if you make your requirements clear to the retailer at the point of purchase and if the retailer affirms that the goods will perform that function.

The goods you buy must also match any description given of them – the year of manufacture, the type, the colour, size, component materials and so on. If you can prove that the goods you bought did not meet these requirements at the time of purchase, you have a claim against the retailer for breach of contract. The retailer may also be in breach of the Trade Descriptions Act 1968.

For sales made after 31 March 2003 you are also normally entitled to legally enforce the manufacturer's guarantee.

If you place an order on the basis of samples of the goods which
you intend to buy (material for a sofa cover, for example), the
finished goods must correspond with that sample. If they do not,
you have a claim against the retailer for breach of contract.

Putting things right

What you are entitled to, if things go wrong with the goods you
have purchased, depends on when you bought them and how
quickly you act.

Purchases made before 31 March 2003

According to the Sale of Goods Act 1979 you have only a 'reasonable' time from the date of sale or delivery in which to reject faulty
goods and receive a full refund of the purchase price (you do not
have to accept a credit note, a free repair or replacement goods).

You are not obliged to take faulty goods back to the retailer: you
are legally entitled to require the retailer to collect them from you.
However, you may find it easier and quicker to get the problem
resolved if you take the goods back to the shop. There is no precise
legal definition of 'reasonable' – it depends on the circumstances
of each case and, in some instances, a reasonable time can be as
little as a few weeks. After that period has elapsed you are entitled
to compensation only, which usually amounts to the cost of repair.
If the goods are still under guarantee, it is probably worthwhile to
claim under the manufacturer's guarantee. And remember, guarantees do not take anything away from your rights under the Sale
of Goods Act.

Purchases made after 31 March 2003

Since March 2003, if you buy something that is faulty, you are *still*
entitled to your money back – if you act quickly – or after that
compensation, under the rules covering purchases made before
that date. But the law gives you new, additional ways of sorting out
your problem.

If you are within a reasonable time since the date of sale or
delivery, you may still demand your money back *or* claim a repair
or replacement. (Although these solutions were often offered,

they previously had no legal backing, so you could not have insisted upon them.)

If a reasonable time has elapsed, you are still entitled to compensation, but you may instead insist on a repair or replacement.

Repairs or the replacement of faulty goods have to be carried out without causing you much inconvenience (including consideration of time taken). Retailers have to foot the bill for any costs involved, such as transportation. However, retailers do not have to agree to repair or replace faulty goods if the cost involved is disproportionate or if repairs, say, are impossible. In these circumstances, you are entitled to a partial or full refund. How much you are entitled to depends mainly on how long you have had the goods and the nature of the fault or problem.

Staking your claim

Before you complain, work out what you are entitled to, and decide whether you want your money back, an exchange, a repair or compensation.

For sales made before 31 March 2003, it will be up to you to prove that goods were faulty in some way at the time of sale. You may need technical evidence from an expert to add weight to your claim. It may be worth contacting the retailer and asking whether he will agree to abide by the opinion of an independent expert. This will save on the costs of both parties getting technical evidence. For sales after 31 March 2003, if a fault appears during the first six months, it will be assumed that you have a good claim. After six months, it is up to you to prove the goods are faulty. This may be difficult if you have had them for some time.

It is, however, important to remember that under your rights laid down by the Sale of Goods Act, the retailer has an obligation towards you for six years from the date of purchase for any breach of contract. This means that even if a reasonable period of time has elapsed, so long as you complain within six years of purchasing the goods you may be entitled to compensation. In Scotland you have five years in which to complain from when you discover the fault.

If you spot a defect in goods straightaway, act quickly: contact the retailer (telephone or go back to the shop) and ask to see the manager. Spell out the exact nature of the problem and how you wish it to be resolved. If you do not receive satisfactory redress initially, write to the retailer reiterating your case clearly, giving both full details of defects in the goods and your preferred resolution of the matter. In your letter, establish a time limit for action by the retailer – for example, 14 days in which to refund your money.

If you ask the retailer for a repair, do so while stating that you are reserving your rights under the Sale of Goods Act. By doing so, you retain the right to claim compensation at a later date if the retailer does not carry out a free repair, or if the repair proves to be faulty.

Rejecting a retailer's denial of liability

Some retailers claim that it is not their responsibility to sort out problems with faulty goods and that the responsibility lies with the manufacturer. Do not be fobbed off. Remember that your contract is with the retailer who sold you the goods. Be persistent, and remind the retailer of his legal obligations under the Sale of Goods Act 1979.

Damage caused by faulty goods

You are also entitled to claim under the Sale of Goods Act 1979 for any damage caused by faulty goods. If, for example, your washing machine breaks down and damages clothes that are in it at the time, you are entitled to claim compensation from the retailer for the damaged clothes as well as for the machine. You can claim only if the damage is caused as a direct and foreseeable result of your being supplied with faulty goods. You will need evidence that items were damaged by the faulty goods, so take photographs if you can, and, if possible, keep the damaged items in a safe place until your claim is settled.

Injury caused by faulty goods

The Consumer Protection Act 1987 states that manufacturers (or producers) are strictly liable if the products they make are defective. If you can prove that a defect in a product caused you personal injury, or damage to your other property over £275, you can claim compensation from the manufacturer, *not* from the retailer. Anyone so injured can claim – the right to do so is not restricted to the purchaser of the goods.

You are entitled to compensation for the time you have had to take off work, lost wages, and the pain and suffering caused by the injury. The amount of compensation you can claim depends on the seriousness of the injury and the nature of the 'loss of amenity'. If you are a painter and decorator, for example, and cannot use ladders for six months, you will be entitled to claim more compensation than someone who does not have to climb ladders for a living. Get legal advice from a solicitor on how much to claim before initiating your complaint.

The late delivery of goods

The law does not normally regard time as a crucial element in contracts for consumer goods. If it is important that the goods you have ordered are delivered to you by a particular date, you should make this clear to the supplier by marking 'time is of the essence' in writing when placing your order. If the goods ordered subsequently do not arrive on time, the supplier is in breach of contract and you are legally entitled to receive a full refund of the price that you paid. And if it costs you more than the price you paid with your order to get the same goods elsewhere, you are also entitled to receive the difference in price from the initial supplier.

If the supplier agrees to deliver the goods but no date for delivery is fixed, the Sale of Goods Act 1979 says that the supplier must send the goods to you within a reasonable time. However, as in other instances, there is no hard-and-fast rule about what is 'reasonable'. It depends on the circumstances – the type of goods, their availability and so on.

Sometimes it is clear, either from a catalogue or from the nature of the goods themselves, that the goods are required by a particular date. If you order goods from a Christmas catalogue, or the goods themselves are particularly seasonal (Christmas cards, say), then it is clear that they must be delivered in time for Christmas. If such goods are not delivered in time, you are entitled to cancel your order and to ask for a full refund of the purchase price.

Mail-order problems

If you order goods through the post or through a mail-order catalogue, you are protected by the Sale of Goods Act 1979. The goods should therefore be of satisfactory quality, be reasonably fit for their purpose and should correspond to their description in advertisements or catalogues. If they do not meet these requirements, you have exactly the same rights that you would have if you bought the goods over the counter at a shop.

When buying goods from a catalogue or from an advertisement in a newspaper or magazine, you are probably covered by one of the mail order protection schemes (see Addresses at the back of this book).

The relevant trade associations will usually investigate any complaint against a member who does not abide by the appropriate code of practice, and they will usually conciliate between you and one of their members free of charge. As a last resort, they usually also offer the option of independent arbitration. You can get copies of their codes of practice direct from these organisations.

Trade associations will also respond to your complaint if a company to whom you have paid money in advance stops trading or goes into liquidation. But there are time limits within which you have to claim, so contact the advertisement manager of the newspaper or magazine which carried the advertisement as soon as possible.

Before placing your order, you should ask the publication carrying the advertisement whether the appropriate protection schemes will cover you if things go wrong with your order. Keep a copy of the advertisement, too. If you paid for the goods with a credit card, you have extra protection if the goods cost more than £100 (see Chapter 10). The Consumer Protection (Distance Selling) Regulations 2000 (see page 31) will also cover mail-order transactions.

Mail-order goods damaged in transit

In practice, mail-order companies which belong to trade associations such as the Mail Order Protection Scheme (MOPS)★ generally agree to replace goods free of charge if they have been damaged in transit. Check with the association to see what is covered by the relevant scheme. You may also have some comeback against a supplier which is not a member of any trade association. If the supplier cannot prove that the goods left its premises in perfect condition, you have a claim to be reimbursed for the cost of the goods.

If it can be proved that the goods were damaged in transit, you have a claim against the carrier. In the case of the Post Office, you should complete form P58 (available at any post office) and send it to the Head Postmaster. Remember to keep a copy of what you write. If you can show that a parcel was damaged in the post, you are entitled to compensation on a sliding scale, but this may not always reflect your actual loss.

Problems when buying goods over the Internet

Buying from UK traders

When you buy goods over the Internet from businesses based in England and Wales you will have the same rights as when you buy from a shop under the Sale of Goods Act 1979. However, the nature of Internet trading can cause additional problems; for example it may be difficult to trace the whereabouts of an Internet trader, making it difficult to get a refund if the goods turn out to be faulty or not as described. If you pay by credit card, however, you have rights against the credit-card supplier (see page 161).

You should check whether a trader belongs to an online code of practice. Each has different provisions but they all aim to set standards for Internet traders to adhere to. These will usually include your rights to return the goods, delivery times and prices.

Because there are several codes, the Alliance for Electronic Business (AEB) and Which? have launched a government-backed scheme called Trust UK★ which sets out minimum standards for online codes. Trust UK provides an 'e-hallmark' which traders can display on their websites, the presence of which will guarantee to consumers that the trader subscribes to a code of practice that meets these minimum standards. Only traders whose code has been accredited by Trust UK can display this e-hallmark. The minimum standards include having in place a complaints procedure, an efficient dispute resolution service, a procedure to guarantee consumers' privacy, and good practice in relation to security of information. Traders also have to comply with the EU Directive which protects consumers in distance contracts (see below).

Buying from traders based abroad

If you are buying goods via the Internet from overseas, the law applicable to the contract (unless otherwise stated) could be that of the country you are buying from. This may differ significantly from UK legislation and may offer different protection. Furthermore, the practicalities of enforcing your rights against a non-UK trader will be difficult and costly and you may not be able to take your claim to a local court.

The Distance Selling Directive

A new European Union (EU) law on distance selling, the Distance Selling Directive, has been implemented in the UK by the Consumer Protection (Distance Selling) Regulations 2000. The Regulations are designed to give basic legal protection to consumers who buy goods and services via the Internet, through mail order, telephone, or any other contract where the consumer and the supplier do not come face to face. However, it does not cover holiday and travel arrangements, or deliveries of goods for everyday consumption (for example, milk). Financial services have their own regulations.

Under the Regulations consumers have the right to:

- basic pre-contract information, such as the name and address of the supplier, the price, and the right to withdraw
- written confirmation of the order
- a cooling-off period of seven working days
- the contract being carried out within 30 days unless otherwise agreed
- a refund of all money taken through fraudulent use of a credit or charge card
- a complete ban on the supply of unsolicited goods and services where supply involves a demand for payment
- an opt-out from receiving spam (junk) email.

Misleading pricing

Under the Consumer Protection Act 1987 traders must not give misleading prices to consumers – for example, all price indications given to consumers must include VAT. A code of conduct gives guidance on good practice. Trading Standards Departments enforce this legislation. The Price Marking Order 1999, designed to implement a European Commission directive, aims to ensure that all EU member states have the same level of protection against misleading pricing of goods. The Order aims to provide price transparency by requiring that goods offered for sale in a shop have an easily identifiable price, without consumers having to ask for it. You should also be able to compare prices easily, since traders are obliged to indicate the final selling price and the unit price of goods sold in quantity.

The law recognises goods advertised for sale in a shop or on an Internet trader's website as simply an 'invitation to treat', i.e. an invitation for you, the consumer, to make an offer to buy which the trader is entitled to refuse. Unfortunately, if the goods have been wrongly priced (for example £5 rather than £500) you cannot insist that the trader sells you the goods at that price. However, you can report the matter to the Trading Standards Department which may take action against the trader for giving a misleading price indication.

On the other hand, if your offer to buy is accepted by the trader before it has been discovered that the item is wrongly priced, and you can show that the contract is concluded through evidence such as an order confirmation, or paying a deposit, then you can insist that the trader supplies you with the goods. If the trader fails to supply the goods, you can buy the same goods elsewhere and, if they cost you more, you can claim the difference in value from the first trader. The trader could try to argue that a mistake had been made which could make the contract void. For this to succeed the trader must be able to show that you must have known that the offer was not genuine. This will be easier to prove where there is a large discrepancy in the price.

Rejecting defective goods bought from a shop

Dear

[Reference: make and model]

On **[date]** I bought the above **[item]** from your shop. On **[date]** it developed serious defects. **[Describe problems.]**

Section 14 of the Sale of Goods Act 1979 requires you to supply goods of satisfactory quality. The fact that the **[item]** showed the above defects **[......]** days after purchase shows that it was inherently faulty at the time of purchase. You are therefore in breach of contract and I hereby exercise my rights under the Sale of Goods Act to reject the **[item]** and to claim a refund of the full purchase price of **[£......]** from you.

I look forward to receiving your cheque for this sum within the next 14 days. If you fail to reimburse me I shall have no alternative but to issue a claim against you in the county court for recovery of the money without further reference to you.

Yours sincerely

Asking a retailer for a free repair to defective goods

Dear

[Reference: make and model]

On **[date]** I bought the above **[item]** from your shop. On **[date]**, **[......]** days after purchase, it developed a serious fault **[describe]**.

Section 14 of the Sale of Goods Act 1979 requires you to supply goods of satisfactory quality. The problem described above shows there was an inherent defect in the **[item]** at the time of purchase, and that it was not of satisfactory quality. You are therefore in breach of contract.

In these circumstances I am legally entitled to financial compensation. However, while fully reserving my rights under the Sale of Goods Act, I am prepared to give you an opportunity to repair the **[item]** without charge to me. Please inform me in writing of your proposals for effecting this repair within the next 14 days.

Yours sincerely

Rejecting goods that are not fit for their specific purpose

Dear

[Reference: make and model]

On **[date]** I bought the above **[item]** from your shop. Before purchasing it, I told a member of your staff that I needed it for a specific purpose **[describe]**. He selected the above brand and model as being suitable for my requirements. When I tried to use it for that purpose, it proved unsuitable **[describe problem]**.

Section 14 of the Sale of Goods Act 1979 requires you to supply goods which are of satisfactory quality and fit for their specific purpose if that purpose is made clear to the retailer at the time of purchase. The problem described above indicates that the **[item]** was not fit for the purpose of **[describe]**, despite your staff's assurances. You are therefore in breach of contract, and I am exercising my rights under the Sale of Goods Act to reject the goods and to receive from you a refund of the full purchase price of **[£......]**.

I expect to receive your cheque for that amount within 14 days. If you fail to reimburse me I shall have no alternative but to issue a claim against you in the county court for recovery of the money without further reference to you.

Yours sincerely

Rejecting goods that do not match their description

Dear

[Reference: make and model]

On **[date]** I bought the above **[item]** at a cost of **[£......]** from you.

When I visited your shop on **[date]** the **[item]** was described to me as follows **[describe]**. It was on the basis of your description that I proceeded with the purchase. I have subsequently discovered that the **[item]** does not match that description and is **[describe including actual value, if appropriate]**.

As your description was a key factor in my decision to buy the **[item]**, the sale was one 'by description', and as the **[item]** does not correspond with that description, you are in breach of contract.

I am therefore exercising my rights under the Sale of Goods Act 1979 to reject the **[item]** and expect you to reimburse me with a refund of the full purchase price of **[£......]** within 14 days.

If you fail to reimburse me I shall have no alternative but to issue a claim against you in the county court for recovery of the money without further recourse to you.

Yours sincerely

NOTE
Remember, you are not obliged to take or send the goods back to the supplier: you are entitled to ask the supplier to collect them, once you have received the supplier's cheque.

Rejecting a retailer's denial of liability for defective goods

Dear

[Reference: make and model]

I wrote to you on **[date]** about the above defective **[item]** bought from your shop on **[date]**. Your reply of **[date]** denied liability for the defective item, claiming that I should complain to the manufacturer instead.

My claim against you is based on the Sale of Goods Act 1979. Section 14 of the Act requires you to supply goods of satisfactory quality. Your failure to supply such goods means that I have a claim against you for breach of contract which is unaffected by any other rights I may have under the guarantee offered by the manufacturer.

I trust that this clarifies the position and I expect to receive your written proposal for arranging for a free repair to the **[item]** within the next seven days.

Yours sincerely

Complaining to a retailer about damage caused by defective goods

Dear

[Reference: make and model]

On **[date]** I bought the above **[item]** from your shop. On **[date]** it developed a serious fault **[describe]** causing damage to my property **[describe]**. This cost **[£......]** to repair.

Section 14 of the Sale of Goods Act 1979 requires you to supply goods which are of satisfactory quality. As the **[item]** is faulty and therefore unsatisfactory, you are in breach of contract.

I am therefore entitled to financial compensation for the faulty goods. However, while fully reserving my rights I am prepared to give you an opportunity to repair the **[item]** without any charge to me.

I am also legally entitled to claim **[£......]** for the **[above damage]** as this cost arose as a direct result of the **[defect]**.

Please inform me within 14 days of your proposals for effecting repairs to the **[item]**. I also look forward to receiving your cheque for **[£......]** within 14 days. If you fail to reimburse me I shall have no alternative but to issue a claim against you in the county court for recovery of the money without further reference to you.

Yours sincerely

Informing a retailer that you are claiming a repair to defective
goods from a manufacturer, while reserving your rights

Dear

[Reference: make and model]

On **[date]** I bought the above **[item]** from your shop.

When I tried to use the **[item]** on **[date]** I discovered
that it was faulty: **[describe]**.

I am sending the **[item]** back to the manufacturer for a
free repair according to the terms of its guarantee.
However, I reserve my rights under the Sale of Goods
Act 1979 to reject the **[item]** and claim a refund from
you if the manufacturer does not resolve the problem.

Yours sincerely

Complaining to a manufacturer about injury caused by faulty goods

Dear

[Reference: make and model]

On **[date]** I bought the above **[item]** from **[retailer: name and address]**. On **[date]** the **[item]** proved defective, injuring me in the process **[describe]**. The result of the injury was **[describe, together with any consequences, such as absence from work]**.

As the manufacturer of the **[item]** which was inherently defective and which caused my injuries, you are liable to me under the Consumer Protection Act 1987 for the personal injury caused by the defect in your product.

I am taking legal advice about the amount of compensation I should claim and will inform you of how much I am claiming in due course.

Yours sincerely

Rejecting goods that do not correspond with samples

Dear

[Reference: brief description of goods]

On **[date]** the above **[item: describe]** was delivered to me. It is unsatisfactory. My order of **[date]** was placed on the basis of specific samples shown to me **[describe: colour, finish, size etc.]**. The item delivered to me differs from the samples chosen in that it is: **[describe]**.

Since the **[item]** does not correspond with the sample I saw and relied upon when placing my order, you are in breach of contract, and under the Sale of Goods Act 1979 I am legally entitled to reject the **[item]** and to receive from you a refund of the full purchase price of **[£......]**.

I am therefore exercising my right to do so and I expect to receive your cheque for **[£......]** within 14 days. If you fail to reimburse me I shall have no alternative but to issue a claim against you in the county court for recovery of the money without further reference to you.

Yours sincerely

Carpet shading: rejecting the retailer's and manufacturer's denials of liability

Dear

[Reference: make and name of carpet]

Thank you for your letter of **[date]** in which you passed on to me the manufacturer's denial of responsibility for carpet shading, on the basis of its being a phenomenon which can occur at random, rather than the result of a defect in manufacture. This argument is unacceptable.

It seems that shading is a known phenomenon which occurs in carpets of the type that I purchased, but you failed to warn me of this possibility at the time of purchase **[date]**. You are therefore in breach of contract under the Sale of Goods Act 1979, and I am legally entitled to redress. While reserving my rights I expect you to replace this carpet free of charge. I look forward to receiving your proposals for effecting this within the next 14 days.

Yours sincerely

Rejecting goods that are not delivered on time

Dear

[Reference: order number]

On **[date]** I placed the above order for **[item]** with you, for which I paid in advance. The **[item]** has still not been delivered.

Under the Sale of Goods Act 1979 you are required to deliver the **[item]** to me within a reasonable time. As **[period]** has elapsed since I placed the order, you have failed to fulfil this statutory requirement and are therefore in breach of contract.

I am now making time of the essence. If you do not send me the **[item]** within seven days, I will consider our contract at an end, as I am entitled to do in law, and will expect you to refund the full purchase price of **[£......]** to me.

If you fail to deliver the **[item]** to me within seven days, I shall have no alternative but to issue a claim against you in the county court for recovery of the money without further reference to you.

Yours sincerely

Cancelling an order for late Christmas goods

Dear

[Reference: order number]

On **[date]** I ordered **[item]** from your Christmas catalogue, enclosing full payment with my order. The **[item]** was not delivered until **[date after Christmas]**, and I was compelled to buy another **[item]** from a different supplier before Christmas at a cost of **[£......]**.

You were obliged by the terms of our contract to supply me with the **[item]** in time for Christmas, and your failure to do so means that you are in breach of contract. I am therefore legally entitled to cancel the contract and to receive from you a refund of the **[£......]**, being the full purchase price of **[£......]** plus **[£......]** postage and packing.

I look forward to receiving your cheque for **[£......]** within 14 days. If you fail to reimburse me I shall have no alternative but to issue a claim against you in the county court for recovery of the money without further reference to you.

Yours sincerely

Rejecting defective mail-order goods

Dear

[Reference: order number]

I placed the above order for **[item]** on **[date]**. The **[item]** which I received on **[date]** showed serious defects **[describe]**.

Under the Sale of Goods Act 1979 you are obliged to supply goods that are of satisfactory quality. The fact that the **[item]** showed the above defects indicates that the goods supplied were not of satisfactory quality, and you are therefore in breach of contract. I am legally entitled to receive from you a full refund of the purchase price of **[£......]** plus **[£......]** paid towards postage and packing, making a total of **[£......]**.

I look forward to receiving your cheque for **[£......]** in the next 14 days. If you fail to reimburse me I shall have no alternative but to issue a claim against you in the county court for recovery of the money without further reference to you.

Yours sincerely

Rejecting mail-order goods that do not match their description

Dear

[Reference: order number]

I placed the above order on **[date]** for **[item]** described as **[quote]** on page **[......]** of your catalogue. The **[item]** which I received on **[date]** differs from the description and illustrations in the catalogue in the following way **[describe differences]**.

Section 13 of the Sale of Goods Act 1979 requires you to supply goods that correspond with their description. As the **[item]** does not correspond with the description given in your catalogue, you are in breach of contract.

I am therefore legally entitled to receive from you a full refund of the **[£......]** purchase price plus **[£......]** postage and packing, making a total of **[£......]**.

I look forward to receiving your cheque for **[£......]** within the next 14 days. If you fail to reimburse me I shall have no alternative but to issue a claim against you in the county court for recovery of the money without further reference to you.

Yours sincerely

Rejecting mail-order goods damaged in transit

Dear

[Reference: order number]

On **[date]** I placed the above order for **[goods]** price **[£......]** as advertised in your **[......]** catalogue. When the **[goods]** were delivered on **[date]** I discovered the following damage **[describe]**.

As you are a member of the Mail Order Protection Scheme, you are governed by a code of practice which states that you will either replace any goods damaged in transit or refund the purchase price.

While reserving my rights, I would like you to supply a replacement **[item]** within 14 days.

Yours sincerely

Claiming a refund from a credit-card company over a problem with goods bought online

Dear

[Reference: account number]

On **[date]** I ordered **[item]** from an e-commerce retailer known as **[name]** at a cost of **[£......]** which I paid using my **[name]** credit card.

The item **[has not been delivered/is faulty]**. The full details of the problem are as follows: **[describe]**.

I understand that under section 75 of the Consumer Credit Act 1974 you, as the credit-card company involved in the transaction, are liable to the customer (me) for any breach of contract or misrepresentation along with the supplier of the goods and services.

The supplier's failure **[to deliver the goods/to deliver goods of satisfactory quality]** is a breach of contract, and as I paid by credit card I hold you liable for this breach. I therefore expect you to credit my account with the full purchase price of **[£......]** within the next 14 days.

Yours sincerely

Complaining to your local Trading Standards Department about misleading prices

Dear

[Reference: business name and address]

I wish to complain about a misleading price indication made by the above business.

On **[date]** I attempted to buy **[goods]** from **[business name]**. The price of the goods was indicated as follows: **[describe price indication]**. However, when I offered to buy the goods and the price was rung up at the till the price indication was false in that **[describe inaccuracies]**.

I understand that it is a criminal offence under Part III of the Consumer Protection Act 1987 for traders to give misleading price indications about the goods they sell to consumers.

I ask you, as the enforcement agency of this legislation, to look into this matter with a view to exercising your powers to stop misleading price indications.

Yours sincerely

Chapter 2

Holidays and travel

When your package holiday booking is accepted (usually by the issue of a confirmation invoice), a legally binding contract is made between you and the tour operator – the company that organises your holiday. The contract is *not* with the travel agent, and if things go wrong, your claim is against the tour operator. On the other hand, travel agents do owe you a legal duty of care and if they do not do a competent job you will have a claim against them.

Descriptions in the travel company's brochure of the hotel and the resort form part of your contract with the tour operator, and are therefore part of your legal entitlements. These descriptions must be factually accurate – this means that the hotel facilities specified in the brochure must exist as described, a 'quiet' hotel must be quiet, and the dates and times of flights must be correctly stated too.

Along with the specific right to features described in the brochure, you also have rights implied into the contract by previous case law, to the effect that the accommodation provided will be of a standard of cleanliness and quality reasonably to be expected from the type and price of holiday booked, so you are in a position to claim if your holiday proves substandard in this regard. Complain on the spot and complete a dissatisfaction report.

Special requirements that you have communicated to the tour operator before making your booking, and which have been accepted by the tour operator and written on the confirmation form, are also part of your contract: so if you have specified a room with a sea view, or a ground-floor room for an elderly relative, for example, you are legally entitled to find them available when you arrive.

Tour operators often put a clause in their booking conditions saying that they do not guarantee special requests. Therefore, at the time of booking you must ask your travel agent to check with the tour operator that your request can be guaranteed. Ensure that it is written clearly on the booking form that your request is a condition of the contract, so that you will be entitled to compensation if the tour operator fails to meet your request.

You can specifically ask the travel agent to act as agent on *your* behalf, instead of as agent of the tour operator, and to make a particular booking on particular terms. If the travel agent does not carry out your instructions when it claims it has, you will have a claim against the agent.

If, when you arrive at your destination, you find that the tour operator has failed to provide the holiday you booked, make sure you complain immediately to the tour operator's representative. The representative may be able to rectify the problem by offering to move you to another room or hotel, for example. If you do not complain and put up with the situation the tour operator can argue that you failed to reduce your loss and this may mean that you are not entitled to as much compensation. Even if the representative is unable to rectify the situation you will be able to argue that you tried to mitigate (reduce) your loss. In all cases you should ensure that you have filled out a customer dissatisfaction report. If complaining at the time does not resolve your problem, write to the tour operator when you get home.

The Association of British Travel Agents (ABTA)★ is the main representative body for both travel agents and tour operators. It operates a bonding scheme to ensure holidaymakers do not lose their money when member companies go bust. It also operates a code of conduct for both tour operators and travel agents which sets standards of service that are binding on members.

Alterations before departure

Tour operators' booking conditions usually reserve the right to make minor alterations to your holiday arrangements without paying you compensation. However, under a European Union (EU) directive, incorporated within English law by the Package Travel, Package Holidays and Package Tour Regulations 1992, if a tour operator makes a significant change to your holiday, it must tell you as soon as possible. You are entitled to cancel and get a refund (and possibly compensation if you suffer additional losses), or opt for compensation. A significant change would be moving you to a different resort. If as a result you choose to cancel your holiday, and it costs you more money to book a similar holiday, you can claim the difference in value as well as a refund.

If despite the alteration you decide to go on the holiday, you should write to the tour operator stating that you accept the alteration under protest and reserve your right to claim compensation on your return.

Remember, any attempt by the tour operator to limit your right to complain or to make changes to your holiday after booking must be fair and reasonable, otherwise you may have a claim under the Unfair Contract Terms Act 1977 or be able to take action under the Unfair Terms in Consumer Contracts Regulations 1999.

Last-minute surcharges can increase the price of your holiday after you have booked – but they are subject to clear-cut controls. Tour operators may not impose a surcharge within 30 days of your departure, and must absorb increases of up to 2 per cent of your holiday cost, but may pass on amounts above this. If the surcharge represents a 'significant' change in the price of your holiday (defined by ABTA as more than 10 per cent), you are entitled to cancel and receive a full refund.

Surcharges can be levied only to recover certain operating costs, such as changes in exchange rates, taxes, duties or fuel prices, and tour operators must explain why the surcharge is being applied. Also, some brochures boast 'no-surcharge guarantees'. These must be honoured, so, where they apply, the price should not increase at all.

Problems after departure

Accommodation

A tour operator's failure to provide you with the precise accommodation you booked is, on the face of it, a breach of contract on the tour operator's part. Under the Package Travel, Package Holidays and Package Tour Regulations 1992, and the ABTA code, operators must take due care to ensure that problems such as overbooking do not happen. However, many tour operators' brochures contain a term in the booking conditions denying liability for changes of plan caused by overbooking, which will probably prevent your claiming compensation so long as the alternative accommodation provided is of the same standard as that booked and is in a comparable part of the resort. But if the alternative offered is of a lower standard, or in a different resort, say, you will be entitled under the 1992 Package Travel Regulations to be repatriated and to compensation if you make a reasonable decision that the alternative is not suitable.

Tour operators' liability for hotels

The Package Holiday Regulations also make the tour operator liable to you for any damage caused by the negligence of any suppliers of the services under the holiday contract, such as hoteliers. So if you become ill by eating contaminated food on an all-inclusive holiday abroad, you can sue the tour operator in this country rather than pursuing a claim against a hotel in a foreign jurisdiction.

If you suffer from food poisoning, seek legal advice. Sometimes, if a number of people become ill, for example, solicitors will bring a joint claim called a 'class action' to get compensation.

Working out your claim for compensation

The amount of compensation you could reasonably expect to receive depends to a large extent on the amount of enjoyment you were able to derive from your holiday. There are four basic components of holiday compensation:

- **loss of value** – the difference between the value of the holiday you got and the one you paid for
- **loss of enjoyment** – something to compensate you for the disappointment and frustration of your holiday going wrong
- **out-of-pocket expenses** – the refund of any reasonable expenses you incurred as a result of the tour operator's breach of contract
- **pain and suffering** – if you have suffered an illness or injury on holiday, you may be entitled to compensation. Consult a solicitor about the amount you can claim.

An example to work through

Opposite we show you how to calculate an imaginary claim: go through the same stages to work out your own claim. There are still subjective assessments involved, and there is no guarantee that the courts will reach the same conclusions if your claim has to go that far – but this at least gives you a starting point.

If you do not achieve a satisfactory result, and your tour operator belongs to ABTA (most do), you have the option of either going to court, perhaps using the small claims track in the county court (see Chapter 17), or using ABTA's arbitration scheme. You cannot do both, and you cannot go to court later if you are unhappy with the result of the arbitration.

The arbitration scheme is run for ABTA by the Chartered Institute of Arbitrators★ to resolve disputes between member tour operators and customers. Which? does not normally recommend arbitration, because it works on a documents-only basis – which means that you have to match the written skills of the tour operator's professional advisers. An oral account of your troubles in court is likely to have a greater impact in your favour. It is up to you, however, to decide which is best for you – going to court or using the arbitration scheme.

1. Take the total cost of the holiday as paid to the tour operator.	Two people paying £1,000: total £2,000	A
2. Was the holiday a *complete disaster* as a result of the tour operator's breach of contract? If YES, go straight to stage 5.	No, it was only the room which was unsatisfactory, and we were out on the beach most of the day	B
3. What proportion of the holiday was ruined? This may involve a number of days which were totally spoiled, or a continuing problem which partially spoiled the whole of the holiday.	We were affected for the first five days of a two-week holiday, therefore 5/14 or 35% of the holiday was spoiled. 35% of £2,000 = £700	C
4. Did you incur any additional expenses as a direct result of the tour operator failing to provide the holiday you booked?	No, none	D
5. Put down an amount of compensation for loss of enjoyment, inconvenience, etc. (It is impossible to calculate this in any scientific way, but courts are allowing quite a lot of compensation for these.)	The unpleasantness of the room, plus the inconvenience of moving to the new one, entitles us to about £250 per person. £250 x 2 = £500	E
6. To get the total amount you should claim, add together amounts C + D + E.	£700 + £0 + £500 = £1,200	

If the holiday was a complete disaster, add together amounts A + D + E

Problems with airlines

Package holidays and charters

If your tour operator changes your flight, look at the booking conditions in the brochure: unless the conditions allow such changes, the tour operator is not entitled to do this. Unfortunately, most booking conditions, and the ABTA code, *do* allow minor changes to flight times. However, you should be given a full refund, or some kind of compensation, if you decide to cancel when the operator makes a major change. In this instance, major and minor are not precisely defined and depend on the circumstances of each case.

Scheduled flights

Under the Warsaw Convention, incorporated into English law by the Carriage by Air and Road Act 1979, airlines are obliged to compensate you if they fail to get you to your destination within a reasonable time of your scheduled arrival. On a long-haul flight, a 'reasonable' time is usually considered to be about six hours. The strength of your claim depends on what causes the delay. If it is a factor outside the airline's control – bad weather, for example – you do not stand much chance of recompense. But if your delay is a result of overbooking, or any other cause within the airline's control, you do have a valid claim and it is worth persisting.

A new EU regulation covering overbooking on scheduled flights from European destinations came into force in February 2005. If you turn up at an airport within the EU and are denied boarding because the flight you have booked is already full, you will be entitled to a full refund of the unused ticket, or a seat on the next available flight of your choice. The airline must also offer you on-the-spot cash compensation: you are currently entitled to about £120 for flights of up to 3,500 kilometres, and £240 for longer flights. These amounts are halved if the airline can get you to your final destination within two hours (or four hours for flights over 3,500 km) of your original scheduled arrival. Many airlines will significantly increase these amounts if you are prepared to accept vouchers. You must also be given a free telephone call to your destination, meals throughout the delay and overnight accommodation if it is necessary.

New rules under the Montreal Convention 1999, which came into effect in the UK in 2004, also increase the potential claim for flight delay to a limit of up to £3,525 where the airline is held to be at fault.

Mishandled luggage

Complaints about lost or damaged luggage are all too frequent. If your luggage is lost, damaged or even delayed on an international flight, you may have a claim against the airline for compensation. Under the Montreal Convention 1999, you can claim up to £850. You will have to prove the value of the contents to make a claim, for example by providing recipts where possible. If your luggage is returned to you damaged, you must make your complaint to the airline within seven days of getting it back. Because compensation levels are fixed, and may not reflect the true extent of a holiday-maker's loss, it is also worth checking your travel insurance to see whether you are properly covered (see page 188).

'Free flights'

In a recent ruling by the Advertising Standards Authority*, airlines which advertise flights as 'free' or costing '£1' have to charge exactly that, with no more to pay. If you come across a flight advertised for a much lower price than what it actually costs, you should report it to the ASA.

Informing a travel agent of specific holiday requirements

Dear

[Reference: booking number]

I wish to book a holiday **[dates, location, price]** as advertised by **[operator]** on page **[......]** of its current brochure. I enclose the appropriate booking form, duly completed.

Please note that I have the following special needs **[describe]** and that I have selected this particular holiday because it offers **[features advertised in brochure]**.

Please ensure that I am booked into accommodation that fits the above requirements, and confirm in writing that this has been done and that the tour operator is aware of my special needs.

I look forward to hearing from you.

Yours sincerely

Complaining to a travel agent about specific holiday requirements not met

Dear

[Reference: booking number]

I wish to complain about my recent holiday, **[operator, dates, location, price]**.

On **[date]** I advised you in writing that I required the following specific features **[describe]**. Your letter of **[date]** confirmed that these facilities would be provided and that they were included in the holiday you booked on my behalf. However, none was provided **[expand if necessary]**.

You were under a legal obligation to book a holiday in accordance with my specific instructions, and to advise me if that could not be done. As you failed to fulfil my requirements, I hold you fully liable for the disappointment I suffered.

Please let me know within 14 days how you propose to resolve this matter.

Yours sincerely

Complaining to a tour operator about a change of specific holiday requirements at short notice

Dear

[Reference: booking number]

I booked the above holiday with you **[dates, location, hotel, price]**.

Today, **[......]** days before I am due to go on holiday, you have advised me that the hotel I was due to stay at has been overbooked. You have offered me alternative accommodation in a different resort or you have offered to allow me to cancel.

It was an express term of the contract between us that I would stay at the **[initial hotel]**. Your failure to provide me with an offer of accommodation at that hotel, or a hotel of comparable standard in the same resort, constitutes a breach of contract.

Since it is too late for me to make alternative arrangements, I am accepting your offer of alternative accommodation under protest. However, I am writing to advise you that I am reserving my right to claim compensation from you for any loss of enjoyment I suffer or additional costs as a result of your breach of contract.

I shall be writing to you further within seven days of my return with details of any claim I may be making.

Yours sincerely

Complaining to a tour operator about surcharges

Dear

[Reference: booking number]

I booked the above holiday with you **[dates, location, hotel, price]**.

Today, **[......]** days before I am due to go on holiday, you have advised me that you are imposing a surcharge of **[......]** to cover your increased costs.

Since the surcharge represents more than 10 per cent of the price of the holiday, it amounts to a 'significant' change to my holiday. I am therefore legally entitled to cancel the holiday and receive a full refund from you.

Please regard this letter as formal notice of my cancellation of the holiday. I look forward to your refund of the full price of the holiday within seven days.

Yours sincerely

Complaining to a tour operator about overbooking

Dear

[Reference: booking number]

I booked the above holiday with you **[dates, location, hotel, price]**.

When I arrived I was told that the above hotel was fully booked and that alternative accommodation was provided at **[hotel, other details]**. I complained immediately to your representative but the matter was not resolved to my satisfaction.

It was an express term of the contract between us that I would stay at the **[initial hotel]**. Your failure to provide accommodation at that hotel, or at a hotel of comparable standard in the same resort, constitutes a breach of that contract. The change of accommodation **[and venue, if appropriate]** ruined my holiday and caused considerable disappointment and inconvenience.

I am entitled to compensation for the consequences of your breach of contract. As I experienced **[problem]**, I look to you to pay me **[£......]** in compensation, calculated on the basis of **[details of calculation]**.

I look forward to receiving your cheque within the next 14 days. If you fail to reimburse me I shall have no alternative but to issue a claim against you in the county court for recovery of the money without further reference to you.

Yours sincerely

Complaining to a tour operator about substandard accommodation

Dear

[Reference: booking number]

I have just returned from the above holiday, which according to your brochure should have comprised **[details]**.

The hotel's facilities, for which I booked and paid on the understanding that they were as described in your brochure, constituted the terms of my contract with you. It was implied in these terms that the accommodation provided would be of a standard of cleanliness and quality reasonably to be expected for this type and price of holiday.

The accommodation was unsatisfactory in the following ways **[details]**. When I asked to be moved to satisfactory accommodation, I was told by your representative that this was not possible; nor were the problems rectified. You are therefore in breach of contract, and I am legally entitled to receive compensation from you. I am in consequence claiming the sum of **[£......]**.

If within 14 days you have not made a reasonable offer of compensation, I shall have no alternative but to sue you in the county court.

Yours sincerely

Complaining to a tour operator about misleading descriptions of accommodation

Dear

[Reference; booking number]

I have just returned from the above holiday **[dates, location, hotel etc.]** as described on **[page ......]** of your **[......]** brochure.

The hotel was misleadingly described. It purported to be **[describe from brochure]** but I experienced the following problems **[describe]**. My complaints to the hotel management and to your representative were fruitless. Your failure to mention **[circumstances]** in the brochure description is misleading, and in law amounts to a misrepresentation. The brochure's description was embodied in our contract and as the description was inaccurate, you are also in breach of contract.

I am legally entitled to receive compensation from you for the disappointment and loss of enjoyment suffered, and for the additional costs incurred. As a result of the problems described above, I incurred the following expenses **[list]**.

I look to you to compensate me with **[£......]**.

If within 14 days you have not made a reasonable offer of compensation, I shall have no alternative but to sue you in the county court.

Yours sincerely

Rejecting a tour operator's unacceptable offer of compensation

Dear

[Reference: booking number]

Thank you for your letter of **[date]**.

Your offer of **[£......]** in response to my letter of **[date]** claiming **[£......]** compensation is unacceptable.

I am therefore writing to inform you that, unless I receive your satisfactory proposals for settlement of my outstanding claim within 14 days of the date of this letter, I intend to issue a claim against you in the county court without further reference to you.

Yours sincerely

Complaining to an airline about flight delays

Dear

[Reference: flight number]

I am writing to you in connection with the above flight, which I took on **[date]**.

The flight was supposed to depart from **[departure airport]** at **[time]**, but did not take off until **[time]** arriving at **[destination]** at **[time]**. When I complained to your staff, I was told that the delay was due to **[reason]**.

It was a term of the contract between us that you get me to my destination within a reasonable time of the scheduled time of arrival. As you failed to do so, you are in breach of contract. Since the delay was due to circumstances within your control, I am entitled to receive compensation from you for the considerable inconvenience caused to me by the delay.

I look forward to receiving a reasonable offer of compensation from you within the next 14 days.

Yours sincerely

Complaining to an airline about lost luggage

Dear

[Reference: flight number]

On **[date]** I was a passenger on the above flight.

My luggage, which was checked in at **[departure airport]**, did not arrive at **[destination]**. The loss was reported to your company staff on arrival and the appropriate luggage report form was completed. I have not heard from you since.

Under the terms of the Montreal Convention 1999 I am entitled to receive compensation from you for my lost luggage. The value of the lost items was **[£......]**. I can provide copies of receipts and other evidence of the value.

I look forward to receiving a reasonable offer of compensation from you within the next 14 days.

Yours sincerely

Rejecting an airline's unacceptable offer of compensation for lost luggage

Dear

[Reference: flight number]

Further to your letter of **[date]** in which you offered **[£......]** in settlement of my claim of **[date]**, I wish to inform you that your offer is unacceptable.

I look forward to receiving your cheque for **[£......]** in settlement of my claim within 14 days. If you fail to reimburse me I shall have no alternative but to issue a claim against you in the county court without further reference to you.

Yours sincerely

Chapter 3

Hotels and restaurants

When you book hotel accommodation or eat out in a pub, café or restaurant, you enter into a contract with the provider of the service. If a dispute arises between you and the service provider, the contract defines the legal status of both parties and gives you rights.

Many of the rights mentioned in this chapter arise from the common law rather than specific pieces of legislation. However, the Supply of Goods and Services Act 1982 ensures that you should receive a reasonable standard of accommodation and service in England, Wales and Northern Ireland (common law in Scotland).

Criminal laws – laws enforced by public authorities – also affect your dealings with hotels and restaurants. The most important criminal laws in this respect are:

- **the Food Safety Act 1990,** covering hygiene in places where the public eats
- **the Trade Descriptions Act 1968,** which ensures that statements in menus and other promotional literature are accurate
- **the Consumer Protection Act 1987,** which prevents misleading price indications generally. In addition, the Price Marking (Food and Drink Services) Order 2003 applies to restaurants and other places where food is served and it states that **all** charges additional to the price of the food must be shown, for example service or cover charges. Prices must also be displayed at or near the entrance so that you can see them before you go inside.

Claiming your rights

If you have a problem, you should try to sort out the matter on the spot. Ask to speak to the manager, explain what the problem is and how you wish it to be rectified – by being given a substitute dish, for example.

If you are not able to come to an agreement with the manager, you are entitled to deduct a suitable amount from the bill. Work out the extent to which you feel your stay or meal was spoiled; for example, if your cheesecake was frozen solid, you could deduct the charge for this. You should leave your name and address at the restaurant so the owner can decide whether or not to sue you to recover the full cost. If circumstances do not permit this course of action, pay the entire bill, making clear that you are paying under protest, by writing words to this effect on the back of the cheque, for example. This keeps your options open to claim your legal rights later.

If you are in any doubt as to your rights, get advice from a Citizens Advice Bureau, law centre or consumer advice centre. The Trading Standards or Consumer Protection department of your local authority may also be able to help. If you go to a solicitor, check first how much it is likely to cost you (see page 204).

When you have found out your legal position, write to the proprietor or manager. Remind him of the problem, and what you want done to resolve it.

A lost booking

When you book a room or table in advance, you make a contract with the hotel or restaurant obliging it to provide you with what you have booked for the requisite number of people at the time you specified. If it does not do so, there is a breach of contract and you can claim a reasonable sum to cover any expenses you incur as a result, such as travel costs.

You can also claim a reasonable sum to compensate you for any disappointment and inconvenience suffered. The amount you can claim will depend on the importance to you of staying or eating at that particular place and the trouble and expense involved in making other arrangements. If the complaint concerns a booking for a special occasion, and the establishment had been specifically chosen to celebrate the event, the amount of compensation that the customer can claim is substantial – for example, if the venue refuses to honour a booking for a wedding party. In this situation you can claim for the cost of booking a similar venue at short notice plus compensation for distress and inconvenience.

However, if you fail to turn up when you have booked a room or table in advance, the hotel or restaurant can claim compensation from you for loss of profit if it cannot then fill the table or room you had booked. Many businesses will ask you to give your credit-card details at the time of booking and may deduct a sum of money if you fail to turn up. However, they must have made every attempt to fill the table or the room, and if they do so they cannot charge you.

Unsatisfactory food

The descriptions of food and wine on the menu form part of your contract with the establishment – 'home-made soup', for example, must be home-made, not canned or from a packet. In addition, under the Supply of Goods and Services Act 1982 (common law in Scotland), kitchens are obliged to prepare food with reasonable skill and care: frozen food must be properly defrosted, for example, and cooked food must not be raw. If you think that the food served to you does not correspond to its description on the menu, or has not been prepared with reasonable skill and care, do not continue eating it. Complain immediately and ask for something else.

If you are not able to have the problem rectified to your satisfaction, you can deduct what you think is a fair and reasonable sum from the bill. Alternatively, you can pay under protest and claim compensation later.

Poor service

If a service charge is automatically added to the bill, this must be clearly indicated both outside the building and immediately inside the door. If there is no indication of the charge you should report the restaurant to the local Trading Standards Department. However, if the service charge is clearly indicated, you will have to pay the charge unless the service was not of a reasonable standard for that type of establishment, in which case you can refuse to pay all or part of the service charge. If, for example, a member of staff has spilled food or drink on you, the service would not have been reasonable and you would not have to pay a service charge. You could also claim the cost of cleaning the clothes damaged by the spillage. The reasonableness of the service is dictated by the type of place you are in and the price you are asked to pay for the meal and service. Service which might be thought acceptable in a roadside café would not be reasonable in the grill-room of a four-star hotel.

If, on the other hand, a service charge is not indicated and not added to your bill, you do not have to pay – it is up to you whether or not to tip, and if so, by how much.

Food poisoning

If you think that the food you ate made you ill, tell your doctor immediately so that you can have a test. Proving who is responsible may be difficult, but you would have a stronger case if more than one person was affected. If you can prove that the kitchen caused your illness, you can claim compensation for your pain, suffering and any loss of earnings and other expenses you incur as a result. In particularly serious cases, get advice from a personal injury solicitor on how much to claim.

You should also inform your local Environmental Health Department. An Environmental Health Officer can investigate the incident and may decide to prosecute; under the Food Safety Act 1990 it is a criminal offence for a business to serve food which is unfit for human consumption.

Other injury and damage

Hotels and other businesses are responsible for your physical safety while you are on their premises. If you do suffer an injury in a hotel, for example, and you think it may be as a result of the hotelier's negligence or that of his staff, you may have a claim for compensation under the Occupiers' Liability Act 1957, and you should seek legal advice immediately.

Stolen goods

Hoteliers owe you a legal duty to take care of your property while it is in their hotel. They are liable to you for any loss or damage to your goods, provided you are not to blame (by leaving expensive jewellery next to an open window, for example). However, the Hotel Proprietors Act 1956 allows hotel owners to limit their liability to £50 per item or £100 in total if they display a notice to this effect at reception. They cannot rely on this limit, though, if the negligence of their staff caused the loss, although you will have to prove this.

Disability discrimination

The Disability Discrimination Act 1995 makes it unlawful for service providers such as shops, restaurants and hotels to discriminate against disabled people. Since December 1996 it has been unlawful for service providers to treat disabled people 'less favourably' because of their disability.

Since 1 October 1999 service providers have been required to make 'reasonable adjustments' to cater for disabled people, for example making changes to the way they provide services or provision of extra help. This could include a restaurant providing menus in Braille or instructing its staff to take the time to read out a menu to a visually impaired person. Since 2004 restaurants and other buildings which are open to the public have to improve physical access, for example providing ramps for wheelchair access. A code of practice describes the duties under the Act and gives examples of what may amount to breaches.

If you believe that a service provider has unlawfully discriminated against you on the grounds of your disability, you may bring a claim in the county court to seek compensation for financial loss and injury to feelings. You may also seek an injunction (in Scotland, an interdict) to prevent the discrimination being repeated in the future (you will require legal advice for this). However, before you begin legal proceedings, raise the complaint with the business concerned to see if the dispute can be settled by negotiation, as the discrimination may have been unintentional. Alternatively, the Disability Access Rights Advice Service (DARAS), established under the Disability Discrimination Act, provides free advice to national and local agencies advising disabled people, such as Citizens Advice Bureaux, but cannot give advice directly to members of the public. DARAS also offers an independent conciliation service to help settle cases.

Complaining to a restaurant about a booking that was not kept

Dear

On **[date]** I booked a table for **[......]** people at your restaurant for **[time, day, date]**. When making the booking, I made it clear that it was for **[details of special occasion]**.

When we arrived at your restaurant as per the booking, we discovered **[problem: details]**. On this special occasion, I was not prepared to wait **[time]** for a table and had no choice but to make alternative arrangements.

Your failure to provide the table booked in advance amounts to a breach of contract, which led in this case to considerable disappointment, distress and loss of enjoyment **[reason why]**. You are in breach of contract, and I am entitled to receive compensation from you for expenses incurred, as well as a reasonable sum to compensate for the disappointment and inconvenience suffered.

I therefore claim **[£......]** compensation and look forward to receiving your cheque for that amount within 14 days. If you fail to reimburse me I shall have no alternative but to issue a claim against you in the county court for recovery of the money without further reference to you.

Yours sincerely

Complaining to a restaurant about an unsatisfactory meal

Dear

On **[day, date]**, my party of **[number]** ate **[meal]** at your restaurant. Our meal was unsatisfactory in the following ways: **[describe item by item]**.

I complained immediately, but after the meal I was presented with a bill for **[£......]** which included the cost of uneaten dishes. I wished to deduct the cost of uneaten dishes as I am entitled to do in law, but was not permitted to do so **[describe circumstances]**. As I had no option but to pay the bill in full, I did so on the express understanding that I was paying under protest and would claim compensation from you later.

It was a term of my contract with you that the food would be as described on your menu, and an implied term of the contract that the standard of food and service be reasonable. You are therefore in breach of contract, and I am entitled to receive compensation for both your breach of contract and the consequences thereof. I was unable to derive any real benefit or pleasure from the meal, so I expect you to pay me **[£...... full price of meal]** in compensation.

I look forward to receiving your cheque for that amount within the next 14 days. If you fail to reimburse me I shall have no alternative but to issue a claim against you in the county court for recovery of the money without further reference to you.

Yours sincerely

Complaining to a restaurant about unacceptable service

Dear

At **[time]** on **[day, date]** my party of **[number]** ate **[meal]** in your restaurant. The service we received was unsatisfactory in a number of ways **[describe]** and we had **[wine, sauce etc.]** spilt on our clothes. The cost of rectifying the damage to our clothes was **[£......]** and in law I am entitled to claim that amount from you as compensation.

I look forward to receiving your cheque for that amount within the next 14 days. If you fail to reimburse me I shall have no alternative but to issue a claim against you in the county court for recovery of the money without further reference to you.

Yours sincerely

Complaining to a restaurant about food poisoning

Dear

At **[time]** on **[day, date]** my party of **[number]** ate **[meal]** at your restaurant. I am writing to let you know that members of my party became seriously ill with food poisoning following the meal.

I have been advised by my GP that the food poisoning almost certainly resulted from the food which had been eaten at your restaurant. This is because **[details]**.

You are legally obliged to serve food which is fit for human consumption under the terms of the contract between restaurant and consumer. Your failure to do so indicates that you are in breach of contract. As a result, we are legally entitled to receive compensation from you for our pain and suffering, loss of earnings and out-of-pocket expenses.

We are taking legal advice on the extent of our claim and will be in touch with you shortly to advise you of the figure.

I have also contacted the Environmental Health Department, which will be investigating the matter.

Yours sincerely

Complaining to a hotel about a substandard room

Dear

On **[date]** I stayed at your hotel for **[number]** night(s) in room **[number]**.

As I mentioned to your receptionist at the time, the accommodation was unsatisfactory in the following ways: **[describe]**. When I asked to be moved to another room, I was told that this was not possible; nor were the problems rectified.

It was an implied term of our contract that the accommodation provided would be of a standard of cleanliness and quality reasonably to be expected from this type and price of hotel. The fact that the accommodation was not of a reasonable standard as required by the Supply of Goods and Services Act 1982 shows that you are in breach of contract.

I am therefore legally entitled to receive compensation from you. In consequence I am claiming the sum of **[£......]**.

If within 14 days you have not offered compensation, I shall have no alternative but to sue you in the county court.

Yours sincerely

Complaining to a hotel about misdescribed facilities

Dear

On **[date]** I stayed at your hotel for **[number]** night(s) in room **[number]**.

As I mentioned to your receptionist at the time, the facilities available at your hotel were misleadingly described in the brochure provided by you before I booked my stay. Your hotel purported to have the following facilities: **[describe from brochure]**. However, I experienced the following problems **[describe]**. My complaints to **[member of staff]** were fruitless. Your failure accurately to describe the facilities available at your hotel and your failure to mention **[circumstances]** in the brochure description is misleading and amounts to a misrepresentation.

The brochure's description of your hotel and the facilities was embodied in our contract. As the description was inaccurate, you are also in breach of contract.

I am legally entitled to receive compensation from you for the disappointment and loss of enjoyment suffered. In consequence, I am claiming the sum of **[£......]**.

If within 14 days you have not made a reasonable offer of compensation, I shall have no alternative but to sue you in the county court.

Yours sincerely

Complaining to a hotel about stolen items

Dear

On **[date]** I stayed at your hotel for **[number]** night(s) in room **[number]**.

While staying at your hotel a theft occurred in my room on **[date]**. The thief got into my room because one of your staff failed to lock the door after cleaning the room. I reported the loss to your staff at the time. However, I have not heard from you since.

You were under a legal duty to look after my property while it was on your premises. The fact that the thief entered my room because your cleaner failed to lock the door clearly shows that you were negligent. Because of your negligence I have lost the following item(s): **[describe]**. I calculate my loss as **[£......]**.

I am legally entitled to be reimbursed in full for the loss of my property. I therefore claim the sum of **[£......]** from you.

If within 14 days you have not offered compensation, I shall have no alternative but to sue you in the county court.

Yours sincerely

Chapter 4

Buying cars

This chapter deals with problems connected with car purchases.

Buying a new car

When you buy a new car from a dealer, you are covered by the Sale of Goods Act 1979 (as amended by the Sale and Supply of Goods Act 1994) and the Sale and Supply of Goods to Consumers Regulations 2002. This means that the car must fit its description, be of satisfactory quality and (if you advise the retailer that the car is for a special purpose, such as rallying) be fit for its purpose. If the car does not meet these requirements, you have a claim against the dealer. If your car is defective, for example, you may be legally entitled to ask the dealer to collect it from you and refund the full purchase price to you. For more details see Chapter 1: Buying goods.

If you decide to reject the car and claim a full refund of the purchase price, you must act as soon as possible. Once you have rejected the car you must stop using it. It is essential to check a vehicle thoroughly when you take possession of it.

Guarantees and warranties offer useful cover. The right kind of guarantee can add to the appeal of buying a specific car. Study the guarantee's wording carefully – certain parts or types of repairs may be excluded. But remember, whatever the terms of the scheme, your rights under the Sale of Goods Act 1979 still stand.

Buying a second-hand car

When you buy a second-hand car from a dealer, you have the same rights under the Sale of Goods Act 1979 as if the car were new. In other words it should fit its description, be of satisfactory quality and reasonably fit for its purpose.

You cannot expect a second-hand car to be in the same condition as a new car, but you are entitled to expect it to be roadworthy. The quality and condition of the car to which you are legally entitled will depend very much on the price you pay for it, its appearance, and any descriptions of it used to sell it to you – 'in perfect running condition', for instance.

When you are buying a second-hand car, you should examine and test it before committing yourself. You may wish to have it examined by a firm of independent engineers. If the examination reveals a defect, or if the dealer tells you about a specific defect before you buy, the dealer is not responsible for those particular defects affecting its performance after purchase.

If a defect which was not discovered when you examined the car comes to light after you have bought it, and you tell the dealer immediately, you may be entitled to reject the car and get your money back. Remember, you have only a short time in which to reject faulty goods.

Many dealers also offer customers the opportunity of buying an 'extended warranty' for second-hand cars. This is basically a type of insurance against mechanical breakdown for a certain period of time or mileage and can be a useful form of cover in addition to your rights under the Sale of Goods Act 1979. However, there may be exclusions which mean you are not covered for the failure of certain parts.

Private sales

When you buy a car from a private seller there is no legal requirement that the goods are of satisfactory quality or fit for their purpose. The only legal requirements are that the seller must own the car and it must correspond with any description given verbally or in writing (such as an advertisement). As it can be difficult to prove later what the seller said, it is best to take a friend or relative along when viewing the car.

Clocking

If the car you bought had a false odometer reading when you purchased it, and there was no indication (a sticker, for example) warning you that the odometer may have been wrong, you will have a claim under the Sale of Goods Act 1979 for misdescription, and also under the Misrepresentation Act 1967 for misrepresentation. This entitles you to cancel the contract and get your money back, or keep the car and ask for compensation. Your compensation will be the difference between the value of the car with its higher mileage and the price you paid for it.

If the car does not match its description (including its mileage), the seller may be breaking the Trade Descriptions Act 1968. This says that it is a criminal offence for dealers to make false statements about the cars they sell. The Act is enforced by local Trading Standards Departments. Since it is a criminal law, the Act cannot help you directly if you want to make a claim for compensation, but it is worth threatening to report the matter to the local Trading Standards Department. This may lead to a quick settlement of your claim.

The problem of clocking is also being tackled by the provision of more information on mileage to consumers. Mileage information is recorded on the MOT test certificate – and the current MOT computerisation project will make this information more accessible in the future. Details of a vehicle's mileage are also requested when a change of ownership is notified to the Driver and Vehicle Licensing Agency (DVLA). This information is also being requested on the forms used when vehicles are relicensed each year. Clocking may also be regarded as an unfair practice by the Office of Fair Trading, who may therefore remove or refuse to grant credit licences to car dealers undertaking such practices.

How to claim

Whatever the problem with your car, contact the dealer about it immediately. Explain the problem and try to reach some sort of compromise. If your problem is not resolved, write a letter of complaint to the manager or owner of the garage, explaining what is wrong and what you want done about it.

Some garages claim that it is not their responsibility to sort out problems with faulty vehicles, and that the responsibility lies with the manufacturer. Do not be fobbed off. Remember that your contract is with the retailer who sold you the goods and that this contract gives you rights under the Sale of Goods Act 1979. So if your claim is rejected initially, or your first letter goes unanswered, be persistent. Remind the dealer of his legal obligations under the Sale of Goods Act.

The law does not require you to take the car back to the dealer; the dealer can be instructed to collect it from you. You should therefore arrange this once you have received his cheque. It may be that the only response to your letters of complaint will be an offer to repair the car under warranty. If this happens, consider this option carefully. The only alternative to a free repair would be for you to sue for the refund of your money. Since a substantial sum may be at stake, you should take legal advice from a solicitor.

Many garages are members of one of the trade associations which adhere to the motor industry code of practice. If the dealer who sold you the car is a member and you are having difficulty achieving your aims, tell the association about your complaint as soon as possible. It may be able to help resolve the problem (see Addresses at the back of this book). If writing to one of these organisations does not resolve the problem to your satisfaction, you have the choice of going to court (see Chapter 17) or taking your claim to arbitration. The trade associations run their own schemes in conjunction with the Chartered Institute of Arbitrators*. Your case will be read by an independent arbitrator who will study your evidence and the evidence of the dealer and come to a decision, but if you are unhappy with the result you will not be able to go to court later.

Rejecting a new car

Dear

[Reference: registration number of vehicle]

On **[date]** I bought the above vehicle **[make, model, engine capacity]** from you. On **[date]** it developed serious defects **[describe]**. An independent examination by **[garage]** revealed that the vehicle had a major defect **[describe]**.

Section 14 of the Sale of Goods Act 1979 requires you to supply goods of satisfactory quality. The results of the inspection clearly show that the vehicle is not of satisfactory quality, and you are therefore in breach of contract.

I am therefore legally entitled to reject the vehicle. I have stopped using the vehicle and it is available for collection.

I look forward to receiving your cheque reimbursing me for the car's full purchase price of **[£......]**. If you fail to reimburse me within 14 days I shall have no alternative but to issue a claim against you in the county court for recovery of the money without further reference to you.

Yours sincerely

NOTE
Under the Sale and Supply of Goods to Consumers Regulations 2002, goods, including cars, purchased after 31 March 2003 will be assumed to be faulty from purchase if they develop a fault in the first six months. This means that it is up to the garage to obtain independent expert evidence to show that the car was not faulty.

Asking a dealer for a free repair to a new car

Dear

[Reference: registration number of vehicle]

On **[date]** I bought the above vehicle **[make, model, engine capacity]** from you. On **[date]** it developed serious defects **[describe]**.

Section 14 of the Sale of Goods Act 1979 requires you to supply goods of satisfactory quality. The fact that the vehicle developed the **[defects]** shows that it was faulty at the time of purchase. It was therefore not of satisfactory quality and you are consequently in breach of contract.

In these circumstances, I am legally entitled to financial compensation. However, while fully reserving my rights under the Sale of Goods Act, I am prepared to give you an opportunity to repair the **[defects]** without any charge to me. Please let me know what arrangements you can make to undertake this work speedily.

I look forward to receiving your proposals for reparation within the next 14 days.

Yours sincerely

NOTE
If you ask for a repair, always reserve your Sale of Goods Act rights while doing so; then, if the retailer does not carry out a free repair or if the repair is faulty, you can still claim compensation.

Rejecting a dealer's denial of liability

Dear

[Reference: registration number of vehicle]

Thank you for your letter of **[date]** in which you deny responsibility for the defects in the above vehicle **[make, model, engine capacity]** which I described in my letter of **[date]**.

I must remind you that my claim against you is based on the Sale of Goods Act 1979. As I pointed out in my previous letter, Section 14 of the Act requires the retailer, *not* the manufacturer, to supply goods which are of satisfactory quality and reasonably fit for their purpose. Your failure to supply goods of the requisite quality means that I have a claim against you for breach of contract. This claim is not affected by any rights I may have under the guarantee offered by the manufacturer.

I trust that this clarifies the situation and I therefore expect you to arrange for a free repair to the vehicle within the next 14 days.

Yours sincerely

Rejecting a second-hand car bought from a dealer

Dear

[Reference: registration number of vehicle]

On **[date]** I purchased and took delivery of the above vehicle **[make, model, engine capacity]** from you. On **[date]** I discovered that it had serious defects **[describe]**. An independent examination by **[garage]** revealed that the vehicle was unfit to drive.

Section 14 of the Sale of Goods Act 1979 requires dealers to supply goods of satisfactory quality. The results of the inspection clearly show that the vehicle was unroadworthy. You are therefore in breach of contract. Furthermore, I was influenced in my decision to purchase the car by the wording of your advertisement **[where displayed]**, describing it as **[quote]**, which gave me to believe that the vehicle was in good running order. The fact that it was not means that you are in breach of the Sale of Goods Act 1979 in misdescribing the vehicle, and furthermore that you are liable for misrepresentation under the Misrepresentation Act 1967.

I am therefore legally entitled to reject the vehicle and to be reimbursed for its full purchase price of **[£......]**. I look forward to receiving your cheque for this sum within 14 days. If you fail to reimburse me I shall have no alternative but to issue a claim against you in the county court for recovery of the money without further reference to you.

Yours sincerely

Rejecting a second-hand car which has been 'clocked'

Dear

[Reference: registration number of vehicle]

On **[date]** I bought the above vehicle **[make, model, engine capacity]** from you. The car had **[......]** miles on the odometer. I have since ascertained from previous sales documents relating to the car that the mileage is substantially greater than this, which suggests that the odometer has been altered.

The Sale of Goods Act 1979 provides that goods must comply with their description. As it was an express or alternatively an implied term of my contract with you that the car's mileage was **[......]**, the fact that the true mileage is **[......]** means that you are in breach of contract. I also have a claim against you for misrepresentation under the Misrepresentation Act 1967.

I am exercising my legal right to reject the car and to receive from you the full purchase price of **[£......]**.

Furthermore, you are in breach of the Trade Descriptions Act 1968 which makes it a criminal offence to give false descriptions and statements about goods. I shall be sending details of this matter to the Trading Standards Department in due course.

I look forward to hearing from you by return of post.

Yours sincerely

Chapter 5

Garage servicing

If you have a complaint about the service you have received from a garage – poor repair work or overcharging, say – take it up with the garage straight away, explaining clearly why you are not satisfied. It may be a question of a misunderstanding that the garage can easily put right. If your problem is not resolved, write a letter of complaint to the manager or owner of the garage, explaining what is wrong and what you want done to rectify it. You should always give the garage an opportunity to put faulty work right, because you are under a legal duty to keep your claim as small as is reasonably possible.

If the garage is unwilling or unable to resolve the problem, and it belongs to a trade association (it is advisable to check this before getting your car serviced), write asking the association to intervene (see Addresses at the back of this book).

The trade associations run their own schemes in conjunction with the Chartered Institute of Arbitrators★. If you do take your case to arbitration, you cannot go to court later if you are unhappy with the result.

A poor service or repair

If you ask a garage to service or repair your car and it is damaged in the process, or fails to function for a reasonable time after the repair because the work has not been carried out properly, then the garage is in breach of contract. You are entitled to claim compensation for any loss or damage arising from this breach, which usually means the cost of getting the damage repaired. However, you should also be compensated for any expenses you incur which were reasonably foreseeable by both you and the garage at the time the contract was made, such as the cost of alternative means of transport while your car was off the road. But you must do what you can to ensure that your claim is kept to a minimum. If you cannot show that you have minimised your loss in this way, you run the risk of not being able to recover all your costs if the matter eventually goes to court.

Overcharging

When you ask a garage to repair or service your car, you are obliged to pay only for work you have authorised. So make sure you know exactly what you have agreed to before allowing the garage to carry out any work, preferably by putting it in writing. If the price is not agreed beforehand, the law says that you are obliged to pay a reasonable price for the work. There are no hard and fast rules about what this is: it depends on the type of repair or service that was undertaken. If you feel that the price you have been charged is too high, you will have to demonstrate that the price is unreasonable, so get evidence in the form of quotations for the same work from other garages, or from a motoring organisation if you belong to one. A useful tip is to ask the initial garage to give you an estimate as soon as the problem has been diagnosed.

If you are forced to pay as a condition for recovering your car, you should make it clear, preferably in writing, that you are paying under protest. This keeps your rights open to seek redress later.

Damage to a vehicle while it is in the garage's possession

When you take your car into a garage for repairs, the garage is legally obliged to take reasonable care of it. If your car is damaged while in the possession of the garage – on the garage forecourt or in a car wash, for example – the garage is responsible, under the law of bailment, for that damage unless it can prove that the damage was caused through no fault on its part.

Garages may attempt to restrict your legal rights by displaying notices denying responsibility for any loss or damage to vehicles left in their possession. Under the Unfair Contract Terms Act 1977 and the Unfair Terms in Consumer Contracts Regulations 1999, notices or conditions in contracts which seek to exclude or restrict liability for loss or damage to property will be upheld *only* if it can be proved that they are fair and reasonable in all the circumstances. It is very unlikely that a court would uphold a garage's claim to be exempt from all responsibility for loss and damage to vehicles in its possession, whatever the cause.

Rogue traders

Consumers often complain that they are 'ripped off' by unscrupulous garages and in the past it has been difficult for agencies such as Trading Standards Departments to take action. However, this situation is likely to improve.

The Enterprise Act 2002 came into force in June 2003. It gives the Office of Fair Trading (OFT), Trading Standards Departments and other designated bodies like Which? a range of powers. This includes the power to take action against rogue traders who harm the collective interests of consumers.

Complaining about the unsatisfactory servicing of a vehicle

Dear

[Reference: registration number of vehicle]

On **[date]** I asked you to service the above vehicle **[make, model, engine capacity]**. When I collected the vehicle from you on **[date]**, I was told that you had carried out a 'full service', had diagnosed **[particular faults: specify]** and had repaired the vehicle accordingly **[specify if necessary]**. The bill for this work was **[£......]**.

On **[date]**, **[......]** days after the service, the vehicle developed serious faults **[describe in detail]**, rendering the vehicle unfit to drive and costing **[£......]** to rectify. A copy of the receipt for that work is enclosed.

You were under a legal obligation to carry out the work on my **[vehicle]** with reasonable skill and care, using parts of satisfactory quality and fit for their purpose, as laid down by the Supply of Goods and Services Act 1982.

The above faults indicate that you failed to do so, and I am therefore legally entitled to receive compensation from you for breach of contract. I look forward to receiving your cheque for **[£......]**, representing **[expenses incurred]**, within the next 14 days. If you fail to reimburse me I shall have no alternative but to issue a claim against you in the county court for recovery of the money without further reference to you.

Yours sincerely

Disputing a garage's excessive charge for vehicle servicing

Dear

[Reference: registration number of vehicle]

On **[date]** I asked your service manager to repair the above vehicle as follows: **[describe]**. I was told that this work would cost **[£......]** but on collecting the vehicle, I was charged **[£......]**.

Since we did not agree a fixed price for this work, I am legally obliged to pay only a reasonable price for the work. To ascertain a reasonable price, I asked two other garages, **[names]**, to estimate the cost of the work. They quoted **[£......]** and **[£......]**, respectively **[£......]** and **[£......]** less than your final bill of **[£......]**. It is therefore clear that your final bill is unreasonable.

In accordance with my legal rights I am prepared to pay only the sum of **[£......]**, based on your original estimate and the two subsequent quotations obtained elsewhere, in full and final settlement.

Yours sincerely

Complaining to a garage about damage to a vehicle while in its possession

Dear

[Reference: registration number of vehicle]

On **[date]** I took the above vehicle **[make, model, engine capacity]** into your garage for a full service. While in your possession, it was damaged as follows: **[describe]**.

You were under a legal duty to take care of my car while it was in your possession. Furthermore, the Supply of Goods and Services Act 1982 requires you to use reasonable care and skill while carrying out work. The fact that the **[vehicle]** was damaged while in your possession is evidence that you failed to take reasonable care of it.

I look forward to receiving, within the next 14 days, your written proposal to effect a satisfactory repair to the vehicle, at no cost to me. If you fail to respond in that time, I shall exercise my common law right to employ another garage to carry out the work and look to you to bear the cost. Any attempt to resist paying such a bill would leave me with no alternative but to issue a claim against you in the county court for recovery of the money without further reference to you.

Yours sincerely

Chapter 6

Property

Problems may arise in connection with property, estate agents and surveyors.

Problems with your new house

The purchase of houses is covered by the legal principle of *caveat emptor*, or 'let the buyer beware': the onus is on the buyer to ascertain the quality and condition of a property before proceeding with a purchase. There are no implied terms in the contract of sale that the property is free from defects, and as a result the purchaser has little comeback against the seller if defects are found after purchase. As purchaser, you do not have the same rights as you have with the sale of goods, such as cars and washing machines, because the law pertaining to the sale of houses does not include an implied term that the property will be of satisfactory quality.

Fortunately, almost all new homes are covered by a warranty scheme which guarantees that they are built to certain standards and that, if they are not, problems will be put right either by the builder, or, where the builder will not co-operate, by the warranty firm. It is very unlikely that you would be able to borrow money for a new home that does not have a warranty.

There are two main warranty schemes for new homes. One is the National House Building Council (NHBC)★ Buildmark scheme, which covers most of the market. Through the scheme the NHBC sets construction standards of workmanship which builders of new properties must achieve, and inspects homes throughout construction. The other, called Zurich Building Guarantees, run by Zurich Insurance★, also offers a ten-year guarantee with similar protection to Buildmark, which can be extended by another five years if Zurich agrees.

Under the NHBC Buildmark guarantee scheme, during the first two years after purchase the builder of the property undertakes to put right any defects which result from the failure to comply with the NHBC's technical standards. You must report any defects to the builder in writing as soon as they are noticed and keep a copy of your letter. For the next eight years, the Buildmark offers cover for any major structural damage to specified parts of the building including the foundations, load-bearing walls and double-glazing failure, and for contaminated land. However, you will not get cover for double-glazing failure or contaminated land if you bought your house before April 1999. If there is a disagreement between the purchaser and the builder, the NHBC may be asked to intervene.

Generally, the guarantee schemes are not a complete guarantee against defects. They are insurance policies which cover specified risks that could be costly to remedy. They do not provide cover for wear and tear or a failure to maintain the property.

Taking a dispute over a new property to the NHBC

If a dispute is not resolved by negotiation between the purchaser of the new home and the builder, the purchaser can ask the NHBC either to conciliate or to arrange an arbitration hearing.

Conciliation through the NHBC Resolution Service is informal and free of charge. An NHBC official will arrange to inspect the property in the presence of the purchaser and the builder. He will decide what work has to be done by the builder and the date by which it must be completed. The builder should then carry out the work recommended by the NHBC official. The purchaser and the builder have to agree to conciliation. If either side does not, the purchaser has no option but arbitration. Similarly, if he is not happy with the NHBC inspector's report, or if the builder fails to carry out the work recommended in the report, the purchaser may apply for arbitration. Under its Resolution Service the NHBC can arrange to do the remedial work needed to put things right if the builder fails to do so.

Arbitration is a much more formal procedure than conciliation and is governed by the Arbitration Act 1996; arbitration is independent of the NHBC, the role of which is limited to administering the relevant application documents when you ask for an arbitration hearing. The arbitrator who hears the case is appointed from the Chartered Institute of Arbitrators★ by its president, who is himself unconnected with the NHBC.

There is no fixed scale of fees – liability to pay costs is decided by the arbitrator. Generally, if the purchaser wins, the builder will pay the costs, but arbitration does need serious consideration, since the cost to the purchaser could be considerable if he loses – he may have to pay the builder's costs, too. Furthermore, the arbitrator's decision is final, and neither party can go to court later if he is unhappy with the decision.

New rules for buying and selling property

The government has made a number of proposals which are designed to make home buying and selling in England and Wales more streamlined and straightforward, and to reduce unnecessary delays and stress. The main proposal requires the seller to prepare an information pack before putting the property on the market. This pack would include documents such as the deeds and lease, search enquiries, copies of guarantees and insurance policies, a draft contract and a survey report. The aim is to reduce the time between offers being accepted and the exchange of contracts – the period when most problems and delays occur. In particular, speeding up the process will leave less opportunity for gazumping – when the seller pulls out to accept a higher offer, leaving the buyer with the wasted expense of purchasing a survey.

The Home Information Pack will become compulsory from 2007.

In Scotland the whole system of land purchase is different and there is less opportunity for problems to arise because once an offer has been made and accepted by the seller, a binding contract exists, preventing buyer and seller alike from withdrawing after this stage.

Estate agents

Estate agents are usually instructed by and act on behalf of sellers of properties. Estate agents' work is regulated by the Estate Agents Act 1979 and regulations and orders made under the Act. The purpose of these laws is to make sure that estate agents act in the best interests of their clients and that both buyers and sellers of property are treated honestly, fairly and promptly. The Director General of Fair Trading is responsible for the working and enforcement of the law. Trading Standards Departments and, in Northern Ireland, the Department of Enterprise, Trade and Investment* are also enforcement authorities. Also, the Property Misdescriptions Act 1991 states that property misdescriptions are unlawful.

If you instruct an estate agent to sell your home, your legal position is governed by the law of contract – it is up to the seller to specify the services required when appointing the estate agent, and to make sure that the agent agrees to perform them. The seller also has rights under the Supply of Goods and Services Act 1982 (common law in Scotland), which states that the estate agent must perform the service with reasonable skill and care. In addition, under the common law of agency, the estate agent is obliged always to act in the best interests of the client. Unfortunately, there are no hard and fast rules about what precisely estate agents have to do to find a purchaser, so when choosing an estate agent you should contact several offices to find out exactly what services are offered.

The estate agent's commission is normally a percentage of the price at which the property is sold. Broadly, the range is likely to be within 1 to 2.5 per cent. Check what is included in the price – photographs, a 'For Sale' board and advertisements in the press or on the Internet may incur an extra charge. The amount you pay also depends on where you live, and on the sort of agency arrangement you choose. You can opt for:

- **sole agency**, whereby you instruct only one agent
- **joint agency**, whereby you instruct two agents. Both have to agree to this, and on who gets the commission on the sale
- **multiple agency**, whereby you instruct as many agents as you like: the one who comes up with the buyer earns the commission. The fee for this type of arrangement will always be the highest.

Before you agree to an estate agent acting for you, the agent must give you specific information about its services in writing. In particular, the agent must give you advance written information about fees and charges. You must also be told about any services offered by the agent to potential buyers – such as arranging mortgages. Any technical phrases used, such as 'sole agency', must be spelt out in definitions prescribed by the Office of Fair Trading

(OFT)*. If you are not given this information in advance, the agent will not be able to enforce payment of fees without a court order.

It is normally advisable to choose a no sale, no fee deal: that way, you pay commission only if the agent introduces you to someone who actually buys your home. Beware of contracts that say that you will have to pay the fee 'in the event of our introducing a purchaser who is able and willing to complete the transaction'. Under this arrangement, you could end up paying a fee if your home was not sold because you took it off the market.

Estate agents are required to reveal promptly and in writing any personal interest they have in a transaction. During negotiations, estate agents must make sure that everyone involved is treated equally and fairly. That means, for instance, that sellers must be given written details of all offers received from potential buyers promptly – except those which the seller has told the agent not to pass on. Estate agents must also tell sellers whenever a potential buyer asks them to provide a service, such as arranging a mortgage. Lastly, it is illegal to mislead buyers or sellers in any way, by giving misleading information about offers, for example.

Your first step with any problem should be to complain to the manager or owner of the estate agent office. If you are not happy with an estate agent, remember that you can take your house off its books. If you do not obtain satisfaction and the agent belongs to a chain, you should then write to the head office. If your problem remains unresolved, you could consider withholding part of the agent's fee. But seek advice from a Citizens Advice Bureau, law centre or solicitor before doing so – you might be sued by the agent, so you should be sure of your position in law.

An agent who is a member of a professional association, such as the National Association of Estate Agents (NAEA)*, the Royal Institution of Chartered Surveyors (RICS)* or the Incorporated Society of Valuers and Auctioneers*, is subject to a code of practice, and disciplinary proceedings can be taken by these bodies. So you could consider pursuing your complaint by those means – but you are unlikely to obtain compensation.

In addition, the Office of the Ombudsman for Estate Agents* has a published code of practice – for example, members must put up a For Sale board only with the seller's permission and agree not to directly or indirectly harass anyone to gain instructions. Under the scheme, the Ombudsman can order estate agents to pay up to

£50,000 compensation to a client. Unfortunately, not all estate agents are part of this scheme; it is operated generally by large estate agencies. Many thousands of the smaller estate agents are not governed by the scheme (though they are eligible to join), so check whether the agent that you have chosen is covered by the scheme before using that complaint procedure. If your estate agent does belong to the scheme, and your dispute remains unresolved, send details to the Office of the Ombudsman for Estate Agents, requesting its involvement in the dispute. The scheme costs you nothing. If your estate agent is not a member of the scheme, your only option is to pursue your claim in court (see Chapter 17). In Scotland, solicitors often sell property and so act like estate agents. See Chapter 12 for more information about your rights against solicitors.

Problems with surveyors

Intending purchasers should always instruct a surveyor to inspect a property before exchanging contracts. The survey should reveal any defects in the property, which could prompt the purchaser to offer a lower price, or even to withdraw his offer to buy.

There are three types of survey available, differing in their depth of inspection:

- valuation reports
- home-buyers' reports
- full structural surveys.

If the purchaser is getting a mortgage to fund the purchase, he will have to get at least a valuation report. Valuation reports are for the lender's benefit, not the purchaser's. They are simply an assessment of what the property is worth and are intended to help the lender decide whether the property represents good security against the mortgage.

If the purchaser wants more information but does not want a full structural survey, he could opt for a home-buyers' report. These reports, on standard forms produced by the Royal Institution of Chartered Surveyors (RICS)★ and the Incorporated Society of Valuers and Auctioneers★, run to several pages and are divided into sections dealing with separate aspects of the structure – main walls, roofs, floors and so on. The report is intended to provide a comparatively detailed, concise account of the property.

Full structural surveys are the most thorough kind and should include a detailed description of the structure of the property, giving an account of all major and minor defects. The report should comment on all the main features of the property, from the roof to the foundations. But bear in mind that it is an inspection, not a test: while the surveyor should comment on things like wiring, plumbing, central heating and so on, he is not obliged actually to test them.

When carrying out the inspection of a property, a surveyor is under a legal duty to exercise reasonable skill and care. If the surveyor does not, and the purchaser suffers loss and damage as a direct result, then the purchaser has a claim for compensation. Strictly speaking, this is calculated as the difference in value between what was paid for the property and its true value in its defective condition.

Some surveyors' reports contain such phrases as 'we do not inspect areas that are not readily accessible' and 'we could not move furniture and therefore cannot report'. These attempts to limit the surveyor's responsibility have to be fair and reasonable. If they are not, they will be invalid under the Unfair Contract Terms Act 1977 and the Unfair Terms in Consumer Contracts Regulations 1999.

If you think that your surveyor has been negligent but he (or his insurance company) contests your claim, you may have to go to court. Negligence cases are often complicated and costly, so you should consult a solicitor – particularly if your claim falls outside the limit of the small claims track (see Chapter 17).

The RICS has an arbitration scheme run by the Chartered Institute of Arbitrators which covers allegations of negligence arising in England and Wales. The scheme is for claims up to £50,000, but the surveyor must consent. There is a £200 (plus VAT) registration fee for arbitration. However, if your claim is for less than £3,000 there are no other charges if you lose. For claims above this you have to pay the arbitrator's costs (up to £1,325) if you lose.

Leasehold properties

Most flats and some houses are sold on leasehold – you own your home for the period of the lease (say, 99 years) and have to pay rent to the freeholder or 'landlord' (or their managing agent). The lease sets out the rights and responsibilities of you and the landlord.

The law in this area is very complicated, and needs to be followed carefully – as the owner of a flat, for example, you could lose your home or have to pay compensation if you break an important part of the lease. On the other hand, as a leaseholder you can take legal action against your landlord if they fail to keep their side of the lease.

Most leasehold disputes are about landlords not maintaining shared parts of a block of flats, or involve high service charges.

Management and service charges

Your lease should spell out the landlord's responsibility to keep the structure, outside and common parts of the building maintained and in good repair. If they or their managing agents do not do this, you can take action to get compensation or to get repairs done.

Leaseholders pay a charge for this service; how this is worked out is normally covered by the lease. Charges often vary from year to year, depending on what is done. You may also have to pay money into a reserve or 'sinking' fund each year to cover the cost of major repairs, such as replacing the roof. But you must be consulted before any major work is started.

Common service charge problems include:

- being charged for things which are not listed in the lease
- uncertainty about who is responsible for particular repairs – and about how the service charge is worked out
- being asked to pay too much
- shoddy work.

Try to sort out problems with the landlord first. If that does not work, you may need to take legal action. Leasehold Valuation Tribunals (LVTs) deal with many common problems, including management and service charge complaints.

For more information see *Buy, Own and Sell a Flat* (Which? Books). The Leasehold Advisory Service★ can give free help on your rights as a leaseholder, and put you in touch with your local LVT.

Complaining to a builder about unacceptable standards of
workmanship in a new house

Dear

[Reference: address of property]

I purchased the above property from you on **[date]**. I
have discovered serious defects in the quality of workmanship used in its construction **[describe]**.

I understand that under the National House Building
Council Buildmark scheme, builders undertake to put
right, in the first two years following purchase, any
defects which result from their failure to comply with
the NHBC's minimum standards of workmanship.

The defects described above indicate that this property
does not conform to these standards. You are therefore
in breach of your obligations under the guarantee
scheme. I expect you to contact me with your proposals
for remedial work within the next seven days.

Should you fail to contact me by **[date]** with proposals
to put the matter right I shall refer the matter to the
NHBC.

Yours sincerely

Asking the NHBC to intervene in a dispute with a builder

Dear

[Reference: builder, Buildmark guarantee number]

I am in dispute with **[builder]** regarding the unsatisfactory standard of the builder's workmanship at **[address of property]**. I enclose all the relevant documents for your information.

As you will see, I have been unable to reach a settlement with **[builder]** and so I now wish to take advantage of your conciliation scheme. I understand, however, that you will first have to write to the builder in an attempt to settle the matter without recourse to conciliation and possible arbitration.

If your intervention fails to bring about a settlement, I would be grateful if you could send me the appropriate application form for conciliation as soon as possible.

I look forward to hearing from you in due course.

Yours sincerely

encs.

Asking the NHBC to arrange for arbitration

Dear

[Reference: builder, Buildmark guarantee number]

Although I have asked **[builder]** to allow the NHBC to conciliate between us regarding the unsatisfactory building of this property, the company is not prepared to do so.

The property has serious defects **[describe]** and I would like the NHBC to arrange an arbitration hearing as soon as possible. Please send me the appropriate application form.

I look forward to hearing from you.

Yours sincerely

Withdrawing instructions to an estate agent to sell a property

Dear

[Reference: address of seller's property]

Further to our telephone conversation of **[date]**, I write to give you formal notice of the withdrawal of my instructions in connection with the sale of the above property.

Yours sincerely

Rejecting an estate agent's claim for commission

Dear

[Reference: address of seller's property]

I have received your letter of **[date]** requesting payment of the sum of **[£......]**, representing **[..... per cent]** commission on the sale of the above property to **[purchasers]**.

We instructed **[another agent]** on **[date]**, prior to our placing instructions with you, and it was on **[date]** that **[purchasers]** first inspected our property. The fact that you subsequently issued particulars of our property to the purchasers is irrelevant, since it was **[other agent]** who introduced them to the property which they eventually bought.

I therefore reject your claim for commission.

Yours sincerely

Rejecting an estate agent's claim for commission, on a 'no sale – no commission' basis

Dear

[Reference: address of seller's property]

I have received your bill dated **[date]** for **[£......]** commission, to which you claim that you are entitled because you introduced **[potential purchaser]** to us who was a 'buyer who was able and willing to complete the transaction'.

It was an express term of our contract that you would be paid commission only if you introduced someone to us who actually bought the property.

As you know, I asked you to take the property off the market on **[date]**. I have not sold it to **[potential purchaser]**, therefore you are not entitled to commission. Please confirm in writing that you have now taken my property off your books.

I look forward to hearing from you within the next 14 days.

Yours sincerely

Rejecting an estate agent's claim for commission on the grounds that no advance information on charges was provided

Dear

[Reference: address of seller's property]

I have received your letter of **[date]** requesting the sum of **[£......]**, representing **[..... per cent]** agency commission on the sale of the above property to **[purchasers]**, plus costs and charges in respect of **[specify]**.

When I instructed you to handle the sale of the above property I was not given any details of the other charges you are now making in addition to your agency fees.

The Estate Agents Act 1979 and regulations and orders made under the Act require details of fees and charges, including any in addition to agency fees, to have been supplied in writing prior to my instructing you. In failing to provide such details you were breaking the law and I am not prepared to pay the sum in question unless you obtain a court order.

I am contacting my local Trading Standards Department about this matter.

Yours sincerely

Asking the Office of the Ombudsman for Estate Agents to intervene in a dispute

Dear

[Reference: address of seller's property]

I am writing about my dispute with **[estate agent – name and address]**, who I understand is a member of your scheme, and I enclose copies of all relevant correspondence, including the particulars that the estate agents drew up on my behalf.

I have been unable to settle the matter with **[estate agent]**, and am therefore referring the matter to you in the hope that you will be able to resolve the dispute.

I look forward to hearing from you within the next 14 days.

Yours sincerely

encs.

Complaining to a surveyor about an inadequate report on a property

Dear

[Reference: address of property surveyed]

On **[date]** your company undertook a **[type]** survey of the above on my behalf, as a result of which I proceeded with the purchase and took possession on **[date]**. On **[date]** I discovered **[problem]** requiring remedial work. The cost of this remedial work has been estimated at **[£......]** and I hold your surveyor, **[name]**, directly responsible for this expense. These defects were present when the survey was carried out and should have been detected and commented on in the report.

Your surveyor was under a legal duty to carry out his services using a reasonable amount of skill and care, and to a reasonable level of competence. This standard has not been met, and I am legally entitled to look to you for compensation, to remedy the defects.

I expect to receive your cheque for **[£......]** within the next 14 days. If you fail to reimburse me I shall have no alternative but to issue a claim against you in the county court for recovery of the money without further reference to you.

Yours sincerely

NOTE
Write to the surveyor before remedial work has commenced to give him a chance to inspect the damage. This is more likely to lead to a settlement of your claim than if you approach the firm once repairs have been completed.

Rejecting a surveyor's denial of liability on the basis of unfair small print

Dear

[Reference: address of property surveyed]

Thank you for your letter of **[date]**.

I am not satisfied by your claim that a clause in your survey to the effect that **[terms of clause]** relieves you of liability in this matter.

The defects that your surveyor did discover **[describe]** should have led him to investigate the property more thoroughly, and to determine the full extent of the **[defect]**. Since he did not do so, the surveyor failed to carry out his services using a reasonable amount of skill and care. Your small print is unfair and therefore invalid under the Unfair Contract Terms Act 1977 and the Unfair Terms in Consumer Contracts Regulations 1999.

I am legally entitled to redress in this matter and I expect to receive your proposals for remedying the matter at no cost to me by return.

Yours sincerely

A 'letter before action' to a surveyor

Dear

[Reference: address of property surveyed]

Thank you for your letter of **[date]**, in which you continue to deny negligence in your survey of the above property.

As you are still not prepared to accept my claim for compensation, I have no alternative but to start court action against you.

Unless I receive your satisfactory proposals for settlement of my outstanding claim within seven days of the date of this letter, I intend to issue a claim against you in the county court without further reference to you.

A copy of this letter is attached for you to send to your insurers as it may affect your insurance cover and/or the conduct of any subsequent legal action if you do not send this letter to them.

Yours sincerely

Challenging unreasonable service charges

Dear **[name of landlord]**

[Reference: address of property]

Thank you for your letter of **[date]** informing me that my service charges for the coming year are **[£......]**. I am very surprised by your letter since the service charges I have paid over the recent past have been as follows: **[give details for appropriate years]**.

I understand that you are entitled in law to recover from me only those service charges which are reasonable. I do not believe the charges you have asked for are reasonable for the following reasons: **[describe reasons]**. I am therefore not prepared to pay the charges as they stand. I am, however, prepared to pay a reasonable proportion.

I look forward to receiving a revised statement setting out the reasonable service charges which are payable on this property.

I hope that we can resolve this matter amicably. If we are unable to do so, I suggest we refer the matter to the local Leasehold Valuation Tribunal.

Yours sincerely

Chapter 7

Building work

Most complaints about building work concern the price charged, the time it takes to do the job or the standard of the work.

Ask three companies to visit you to estimate the cost of the work, and discuss the job in detail with each builder when he visits your house to inspect the site. Make sure each builder is given the same information upon which to base a quote. If at all possible, use a builder recommended by a friend or relative. Also ask to see work done for other clients, and talk to them about the quality of the builder's work.

Major building work

If you are considering major building work, it can pay to instruct an architect. When you do this, the architect is placed under a legal responsibility to carry out the work with due care, skill and diligence. If the architect fails to exercise the requisite degree of skill and care, causing you to suffer loss or damage as a direct and foreseeable result, you have a claim for breach of contract.

What is required to fulfil the standard of reasonable skill and care varies according to the facts of each case. However, the starting point is always the relevant contracts. It is also relevant to look at the surrounding circumstances. There are various codes of practice governing the professions. These broadly reflect good practice; departure from them adds to your ammunition.

The Defective Premises Act 1972 also imposes legal duties on those involved in the design or construction of homes – builders, developers, contractors, architects, surveyors and so on. It lays down that they must see that the work they take on is done in a workmanlike or professional manner, with proper materials. If they don't, householders can claim under the Act. However, the cover provided by the Act is limited. A claim exists only if the defects in the home cause it to be unfit for habitation as a result of failures in design, workmanship or materials. So, many serious defects such as uneven floors, defective finishes or leaky windows might not fall within the protection given by the Act.

Also, improvement works, refurbishment and some minor types of conversion work are not covered by the Act; nor does it cover work carried out on or to an existing dwelling, falling short of the provision of the dwelling itself.

Estimates

A builder may give you a provisional price or a firm one. If the document he provides gives precise details of the work with detailed costs, the price should be binding on him. A rough price is only a general guide: when he eventually sends you his bill, the builder may charge you more. Normally, a builder's **estimate** is a rough, provisional guide to the price that will be charged when the work is complete; a **quotation** is a fixed price. If you do not agree a price in advance, you are legally obliged to pay a 'reasonable' price. What is reasonable depends on how much work has been done and the type of job that was undertaken.

Have a proper written contract drawn up between yourself and the builder, particularly for major, costly jobs. By doing so, it makes it easier to prove exactly what you and the builder agreed should any problem arise. Various organisations, such as the Joint Contracts Tribunal★, produce standard contracts. The Royal Institute of British Architects (RIBA)★ also publishes a standard form of contract called 'Small Works SW/99' (you can request this from architects).

A typical simple contract which you draw up yourself should include:

- your name and the name of the builder
- the standard of workmanship and materials to be used, including a statement that the work will be in accordance with any given plans and specifications: these specifications may refer to appropriate British Standards or Codes of Practice
- the date on which the work will be started
- the date on which the work will be finished. You may also include a clause stating that the builder will pay you reasonable compensation if the completion is delayed. You should specify a

degree of flexibility as regards the completion date, due to delays being caused by unusually bad weather or other circumstances beyond the builder's control

- a clause to the effect that the builder should leave the site in a tidy state at the end of the work
- clarification as to which party is responsible for obtaining planning permission
- precise details of how changes to specifications will be agreed
- a stipulation that the builder will be properly insured
- a precise definition of circumstances in which you or the builder can terminate the contract
- the total cost of the work and how the bill will be paid – in a lump sum at the end, or in stage payments as the work progresses
- a requirement that the builder return to put right any defects that manifest themselves in the work after it is completed, and to rectify any damage caused to your property, at his expense
- a requirement that in the event of a dispute over the cause of any defects you may appoint an expert to report on the faulty work and/or materials and the builder will agree to accept the findings of that expert and, if the report proves the liability of the builder for the faulty work and/or materials, the builder agrees to pay the cost of that report.

If the builder offers his own contract for the work, you should read its small print very carefully and check it against this list before signing. If the builder has reservations about the contract you want to use, discuss it to see if you can reach a sensible compromise.

Coping with delays

If it is important to you that the work is completed by a particular date, get the builder to agree in writing to a specific date for completion of the work, and also make clear in writing that 'time is of the essence'. By doing so you give yourself stronger legal rights in the event of the work not being finished on time – if the builder does not complete the job on time, you could, for example, cancel the contract and call in another builder to complete the work; if this costs you more than the first builder's estimate, you can claim the extra cost from the original firm.

The law does not normally regard time as a crucial element of building contracts, so if the work is not done on time, and you have not agreed that time is of the essence, you may claim compensation for breach of contract if you have suffered financially as a result of the delay – for example you have been compelled to eat out because of the unfinished state of your kitchen – but the contract will still stand and you will not be entitled to call in another builder to finish the job.

If you have not agreed a completion date, you are entitled to have the work carried out within a reasonable time. This period is not defined by law but it depends on the size and type of work involved. So if the work is delayed you should give the builder written notice that you are making time of the essence and fix a reasonable date for completion. Then if the work is not finished on time you can safely consider the contract at an end.

Faulty workmanship

Every time a builder agrees to carry out work for a client, the client enters into a contract with him. Along with the specific rights given in the contract (for example, the types of materials that the builder should use) the client also has rights under the Supply of Goods and Services Act 1982 (common law in Scotland), which entitle the client to have the work carried out with reasonable skill and care, and within a reasonable time. If the builder does not carry out work as specifically agreed in the contract (if he uses the wrong type of roof tiles, for example) or does not carry out the work with reasonable skill and care, the client can claim for breach of contract. This means that he is legally entitled to have the work put right free of charge.

Calling in another contractor

If the builder does not put the work right, the client should get two or three quotations for remedying the problem and send these to the first builder. This shows he is serious and will, if necessary, call in another builder to carry out remedial work.

Getting the cost back

If the client eventually has to get another firm to put the work right, he is legally entitled to claim the cost of this firm's work from the original firm. But he may need evidence from an expert to substantiate his claim. He can get this from the firm that does the repairs, by asking the repairer for a written diagnosis of what was wrong.

Rogue builders

In June 2003 the Enterprise Act 2002 came into force. The Act strengthens consumer protection in cases where rogue traders, including builders, harm the collective interests of consumers.

The Act provides:

- power for the courts to grant injunctions against specific practices carried out by certain named traders
- power for the courts to ban from trading for a period traders with a record of disregarding their legal obligations
- new powers for Trading Standards Departments making it easier to control trading practices at a local level.

If you are looking for a builder, and want to avoid the cowboys, help is finally on its way. In June 2000, the government launched a register of builders who meet minimum standards of skill, workmanship, qualification and financial stability. Consumers can use the register to find a reputable builder who has been awarded the Quality Mark: see (*www.qualitymark.org.uk*). Approved builders should also offer an insurance-backed warranty, covering the consumer against poor workmanship and builder insolvency. Linked to this, the builder will be required to belong to an effective complaints and discipline procedure.

To apply for the mark, builders have to submit references from satisfied customers, and their work may be inspected as part of the application process. To keep them on their toes, builders also have to re-register each year. And consumers using a Quality Mark builder are covered by a warranty against shoddy workmanship or the builder going bust. There is also a complaints system to resolve any disputes.

See also *Getting the Best From Your Builder* (Which? Books).

Asking a builder to submit an estimate for a job

Dear

[Reference: brief description of job]

Further to our telephone conversation of **[date]**, I would like you to give me an estimate for **[precise details of service required]** at **[address]**.

Please confirm a date and time for your visit to undertake a detailed estimate.

I look forward to hearing from you within the next seven days.

Yours sincerely

Rejecting a builder's bill for more than the original quotation

Dear

[Reference: quotation number]

I was surprised to see from your invoice **[number]** of **[date]** that the cost of **[work and fittings: describe]** is **[£......]**, **[£......]** higher than that in your firm's original quotation of **[£......]** of **[date]**, which set out the fixed price for the work and which was the basis upon which I entered into a contract with you.

Though you claim the increase is due to **[factors, describe]**, this has no bearing on our contract. There was no agreement between us at the time I commissioned your firm to carry out the work that I should bear the cost of **[external factors: describe if appropriate]**. We agreed an exact price for the work and therefore my contractual obligation is simply to the contracted price shown in your quotation.

I therefore enclose a cheque for **[£......]**, being the amount of the original quotation, in full and final settlement.

Yours sincerely

enc.

Complaining to a builder about delays in completing a job

Dear

[Reference: estimate number]

I am extremely concerned about your delay in completing the **[work]** contracted for the above property **[address if different from letterhead]**.

Prior to my accepting your estimate for the job, I was assured that the work would be completed by **[date]**. **[......]** weeks/months later, the work is incomplete **[details of work still to be done]**.

I am therefore making time of the essence in this contract. If your firm does not complete the outstanding work within 14 days of the date of this letter, I shall consider the contract between us to be at an end, as I am legally entitled to do. I shall then instruct another firm to complete the work, deducting the cost from the balance requested in your invoice.

Yours sincerely

Responding to a builder's continued failure to complete work on time

Dear

[Reference: estimate number]

Further to my letter of **[date]**, in which I made time of the essence, I am disappointed that you have not replied to my letter and have failed to complete the work in the time stipulated.

In the circumstances I am left with no alternative but to consider our contract at an end.

In accordance with my legal rights, I now intend to have the work completed by another contractor at your expense. I am therefore obtaining estimates from other contractors and shall forward copies to you in due course.

Yours sincerely

Deducting the cost of subsequent builder's work from the initial builder's bill

Dear

[Reference: estimate number]

On **[date]** I sent you **[......]** estimates from builders who were prepared to complete the work left unfinished by your company. Since you have not responded to any of my letters, I was compelled to engage **[contractor]**, who provided the lowest estimate. The bill for completing the job was **[£......]**.

Since I incurred this expenditure as a direct result of your breach of contract, I am legally entitled to look to you to meet the cost of the work. I am therefore deducting **[£......]** from the balance of **[£......]** due to your firm.

I enclose a cheque for **[£......]** in full and final settlement for the work your company carried out on my property.

Yours sincerely

enc.

Asking a builder to rectify his defective workmanship

Dear

[Reference: estimate number]

On **[date]** you undertook **[work]** at the above address. On **[date]** this work proved defective: **[describe]**.

It was implied in the contract between us that you would carry out the work with reasonable skill and care and would use materials of a reasonable quality. This is laid down by the Supply of Goods and Services Act 1982. The above defect shows that you have failed to fulfil these legal obligations. I therefore have a claim against you for breach of contract.

However, while reserving my rights to claim against you, I am prepared to give you an opportunity to carry out repairs to rectify the matter within a reasonable time at no charge to me.

If you do not carry out the necessary remedial work within 14 days, I shall have no alternative but to retain another contractor to put the matter right and look to you to bear the cost of the work, as I am legally entitled to do.

Yours sincerely

NOTE
When you give the builder a chance to put the work right, make sure you keep your rights open by saying at the outset that you are 'reserving your rights'. That way you can still claim if the job is done badly.

Informing a builder that you are appointing another builder to rectify his defective workmanship

Dear

[Reference: estimate number]

Since you have failed to carry out the repairs to my property within the time specified in my letter of **[date]**, I have had no alternative but to obtain estimates from other contractors, namely **[contractors]**; copies of these estimates are enclosed.

As you will see, the estimates show that the work you did **[describe]** is defective and needs extensive repair. These repairs will cost at least **[£......]**, as indicated on the lowest of the **[......]** estimates. I am legally entitled to expect you to pay for this work, and I therefore look forward to receiving your proposals for settlement by return.

Yours sincerely

encs.

Claiming the cost of subsequent repairs from a builder whose workmanship was defective

Dear

[Reference: estimate number]

Since you failed to reply to my letter of **[date]**, I had no alternative but to engage **[contractor]** to carry out the remedial work necessitated by the substandard nature of your original work. That work is now complete and has cost **[£......]**. A copy of the firm's invoice is enclosed for your information.

You will also see that I have enclosed a copy of a report I asked **[contractor]** to prepare on the work required, which shows that the work carried out by you was substandard. As it was not carried out with due skill, I have a claim against you for breach of contract. In the circumstances I am exercising my legal right to expect you to reimburse me with the cost of repairs, **[£......]**.

I look forward to receiving your cheque within the next 14 days. If you fail to reimburse me I shall have no alternative but to issue a claim against you in the county court for recovery of the money without further reference to you.

Yours sincerely

encs.

NOTE
If this does not settle the claim, send a letter before action (see page 128), threatening court action (see Chapter 17).

Sending a builder a letter before action

Dear

[Reference: estimate number]

Further to my letter of **[date]**, to which you have not replied, I write to inform you that, unless I receive your satisfactory proposals for settlement of my outstanding claim within seven days of the date of this letter, I intend to issue a claim against you in the county court, without further reference to you.

Yours sincerely

NOTE
If this letter does not resolve the matter and the sum involved is under £5,000 (£2,000 in Northern Ireland, £750 in Scotland) (see Chapters 18 and 19), issue a claim in the small claims track (see Chapter 17); otherwise consult a solicitor.

Complaining about work carried out by an architect

Dear

[Reference: address where work is taking place]

I am writing to complain about the service you provided when I instructed you to prepare the following plans **[describe]** for, and supervise the work at, the above address.

When I first spoke to you on **[date]**, I made it clear that I wanted the work to proceed as follows **[describe]**. It has now become apparent that the service you have provided is deficient in the following respects **[describe]**.

The Royal Institute of British Architects' standard form of contract covering our agreement, 'Small Works SW/99', provides as follows **[set out specific clauses that the architect has not followed]**. Also, the Supply of Goods and Services Act 1982 requires you to carry out your service as an architect with reasonable skill and care. The problems described above show that you failed in your legal obligations. I therefore have a claim against you for breach of contract.

Because of your breach of contract I have suffered the following loss **[describe]**.

I consider that **[£......]** would be a reasonable sum of compensation for your failure to meet your legal obligations. I therefore look forward to receiving your cheque within the next 14 days.

Yours sincerely

Complaining to an architect under the Defective Premises Act

Dear

[Reference: address where work is taking place]

I am writing to complain about the service you provided when I instructed you to prepare the following plans **[describe]** for, and supervise the work at, the above address.

When I first spoke to you on **[date]**, I made it clear that I wanted the work to proceed as follows **[describe]**.

The Defective Premises Act 1972 also imposes a legal duty on you to see that the work was done in a workmanlike or professional manner, with proper materials. Also, the Supply of Goods and Services Act 1982 requires you to carry out your service as an architect with reasonable skill and care.

The problems and defects described above have caused my home to be unfit for habitation. This clearly shows that you have failed in your legal obligations. I therefore have a claim against you for breach of contract.

Because of your breach of contract I have suffered the following loss **[describe]**.

I consider that **[£......]** would be a reasonable sum of compensation for your failure to meet your legal obligations. I therefore look forward to receiving your cheque within the next 14 days.

Yours sincerely

Chapter 8

Commercial services

You can take steps to deal with difficulties you may encounter when using certain commercial services.

Dry-cleaners

The Supply of Goods and Services Act 1982 (common law in Scotland) entitles you to have dry-cleaning carried out with reasonable skill and care. If the dry-cleaner provides a service which does not meet these standards, you can claim compensation. Generally, you are entitled to claim the cost of replacing the damaged or missing item, though you may find that the amount of compensation is reduced to take into account wear and tear of the garment.

If a problem arises, write to the dry-cleaner in the first instance. If this does not sort out the problem, but the firm belongs to the Textile Services Association (TSA Ltd)*, write to that body. If your clothes have been damaged or unsatisfactorily processed due to the dry-cleaner's negligence, the association may conciliate between you and the dry-cleaners in your claim for compensation. TSA Ltd also offers an arbitration service based on reports by independent test houses, paid for on a 'loser pays' basis.

If the firm is not a member of the TSA or fails to offer compensation, pursue the matter through the small claims track in the county court.

Photoprocessors

The Supply of Goods and Services Act 1982 (common law in Scotland) gives you rights when you have films processed. If your photographs of a once-in-a-lifetime holiday, for example, are lost or damaged by a photoprocessor, you are entitled to claim compensation for the value of the film and for the loss of enjoyment which you would have had from the photographs had they been processed correctly. The amount of compensation to claim depends upon the importance to you of the photographs that have been lost or damaged. You will get more compensation for lost films of your own wedding, for example, than for those of a distant relative's birthday celebrations. The loss of photographs of your silver wedding or of your child receiving the gold award in the Duke of Edinburgh's award scheme could result in your receiving compensation of around £200 at current values. If the photographs are not of a unique event and their subject can easily be photographed again, you are entitled to claim only the cost of a replacement film and the cost of postage.

Photoprocessors often claim that they are not liable to pay compensation, alleging that their obligations are limited by the terms of the small print on the film's packaging. Do not be deterred by this argument. To be legally binding small print has to be fair and reasonable, as laid down by the Unfair Contract Terms Act 1977 and the Unfair Terms in Consumer Contracts Regulations 1999. Most photoprocessors now use small print which says that films that are very valuable to you may be processed separately for an extra charge, or which advises you to take out your own insurance. The reasonableness, in the legal sense, of these clauses depends on the size and legibility of the small print and the alternative sorts of services offered by the firm to consumers.

Removal companies

When you instruct a removal company to move your household possessions, you are entitled to have the service performed with reasonable skill and care. This is laid down by the Supply of Goods and Services Act 1982 (common law in Scotland). If the company does not carry out the service properly – if crockery packed by its staff gets broken, for example – you are legally entitled to claim against the firm for breach of contract.

Broken appointments
If you instruct a removal company to collect your possessions at a precise time and date, and it fails to turn up on time or at all,

despite having agreed to do so, you have a claim against it for breach of contract. You are entitled to cancel the contract and to hire another removal company to move your possessions.

Removal firms have a trade association, the British Association of Removers (BAR)★, which aims to resolve complaints against its members by conciliating between the parties involved, if they agree to it. It will also appoint an independent arbitrator if both parties agree to it.

Hairdressers and beauticians

Hairdressers and beauticians provide a service. Again, the Supply of Goods and Services Act 1982 (common law in Scotland) entitles you to have the service performed with reasonable skill and care and with materials of a reasonable quality. So, when carrying out a chemical treatment to your hair, for example, a competent hairdresser should first carry out a patch test on a small section of your scalp to test for any adverse reaction. If the hairdresser does not do this and you suffer injury as a result, you have a claim for compensation for pain and suffering and any other loss you have suffered as a result.

If your complaint is about a serious problem, take photos of what has gone wrong and the injuries you have suffered. Also, get a GP's opinion backing your case. If the problem is particularly serious, you may be referred to a specialist, such as a dermatologist or a trichologist. If you have suffered serious injuries you should consult a personal injury solicitor who will be able to assess how much compensation you can claim. Accident Line★ (a scheme endorsed by The Law Society★) can put you in touch with a solicitor in your area who specialises in personal injury. Solicitors who are members of the Accident Line scheme will give you a free interview to assess the merits of your case. You can pursue personal injury claims worth less than £1,000 yourself through the small claims track of the county court in England and Wales.

If the hairdresser with whom you are unable to sort out a complaint is a member of the Hairdressing Council★ (look in the salon for a logo), you can write to this organisation because it has the power to deregister a hairdresser and the threat of this may help speed up the settlement of your dispute.

Complaining to a dry-cleaner about damage caused by its service

Dear

I am writing about the damage to **[item: type, make, fabric, colour etc.]** caused by your establishment on **[date]**.

The Supply of Goods and Services Act 1982 requires you to carry out your service as a dry-cleaner in a good and workmanlike manner, using that degree of skill and care reasonably to be expected from a firm purporting to be experienced in the work. The damage to the above item **[describe]** is evidence that you have failed to exercise your duty when undertaking cleaning on my behalf.

You are required by law to compensate me for my loss and I therefore look forward to receiving your proposals for settlement within 14 days.

Yours sincerely

Asking the Textile Services Association to intervene in a dispute with a dry-cleaner

Dear

[Reference: dry-cleaning establishment]

I am in dispute with the above company over the damage caused to **[item]** when in its possession. I enclose copies of all the relevant correspondence.

As I have been unable to reach a settlement with **[establishment]** I now wish to take advantage of your advisory and conciliation service.

I therefore look forward to hearing from you in due course.

Yours sincerely

encs.

Claiming compensation from a photoprocessor for damaged photographs

Dear

On **[date]** I sent you **[description of film]** for processing, but it was damaged **[describe how]** while in your possession.

The ruined photographs represented **[describe]** and by the nature of the event are irreplaceable.

Under the Supply of Goods and Services Act 1982 you were obliged to ensure that the film was processed with reasonable skill and care. The above damage shows that you failed to meet your legal obligations.

I am legally entitled to receive compensation from you for the value of the film and for the loss of enjoyment which would have been derived from the record of this once-in-a-lifetime event.

I consider that **[£......]** would be a reasonable sum of compensation for your failure to meet your legal obligations. I therefore look forward to receiving your cheque within the next 14 days.

Yours sincerely

Rejecting a photoprocessor's unacceptable offer of compensation

Dear

Thank you for your letter of **[date]** offering me **[terms of compensation]**.

I am not prepared to accept your offer, and I reject your claim that your obligations are limited by the small print on the packaging of your films. As the small print on the mailing envelope was almost illegible and did not make it clear that different types of service were available, it was unfair and unreasonable and ineffective, as defined by the Unfair Contract Terms Act 1977 and the Unfair Terms in Consumer Contracts Regulations 1999.

I am therefore entitled to receive proper compensation for the damaged films, and I expect you to pay me the **[£......]** that I claimed in my letter of **[date]**, within the next 14 days.

Yours sincerely

NOTE
If the photoprocessor still fails to settle your claim, your only option is to pursue the matter in the county court (see Chapter 17).

Complaining to a removal company about damage to possessions caused in transit

Dear

[Reference: removal order number]

I am writing to you about the damage to **[property: describe]** caused when you moved my possessions from **[location]** to **[location]** on **[date]** which I pointed out to your staff when my possessions were unloaded.

The Supply of Goods and Services Act 1982 requires you to carry out your services with reasonable skill and care. The above damage indicates that you failed to fulfil these legal obligations when undertaking the work. I therefore have a claim against you for breach of contract.

However, while reserving my rights, I am prepared to give you an opportunity to arrange for the necessary remedial work to restore the **[items]** to their former good condition within a reasonable time.

Please let me know within the next 14 days what arrangements you intend to make to remedy your breach of contract.

Yours sincerely

Complaining to a removal company about its failure to keep an appointment

Dear

[Reference: removal order number]

On **[date]** I made a booking with your firm to collect items from **[location]** at **[time]** on **[date]** and deliver to **[location]** on **[date]**.

Your failure to collect at the agreed time constitutes a breach of contract. I am therefore entitled to claim compensation from you not only for my out-of-pocket expenses **[describe]**, but also for the substantial inconvenience I suffered in having to make alternative arrangements for this delivery to take place **[describe]**.

In the circumstances, I expect to receive compensation of **[£......]** within 14 days.

Yours sincerely

Complaining to a hairdresser about damage to your hair

Dear

I am writing to you about the damage to my scalp and hair caused by you when you **[describe treatment]**. Shortly after I received the treatment, it became apparent that I was suffering from the following problems **[describe]**.

The Supply of Goods and Services Act 1982 requires you to carry out your service as a hairdresser with reasonable skill and care, using materials of a reasonable quality. The problems described above show that you failed in your legal obligations. I therefore have a claim against you for breach of contract.

Because of your breach of contract I have suffered the following injuries **[describe, together with any consequences, such as medical treatment, absence from work and so on]**.

I consider that **[£......]** would be a reasonable sum of compensation for your failure to meet your legal obligations. I therefore look forward to receiving your cheque within the next 14 days.

Yours sincerely

Asking the Hairdressing Council to intervene in a dispute with a hairdresser

---

Dear

[Reference: name of salon]

I am in dispute with the above named salon concerning the service I received from it on **[date]**.

I enclose copies of the relevant correspondence. As you will see, the treatment I received from the salon caused the following injuries **[describe, together with any consequences, such as medical treatment, absence from work and so on]**.

I contacted the salon on **[date]** to complain about this matter but the dispute has not been resolved to my satisfaction.

Since the salon is a member of the Council I am now referring the matter to you for consideration. I look forward to hearing from you in due course.

Yours sincerely

encs.

Chapter 9
Utilities

The electricity, gas and telecommunications markets have experienced an increase in competition as new suppliers vie for a share of the market, and consumers now have a range of suppliers from which to choose. However, at present you have no choice in which company supplies your water and sewerage services, though this may change in the future.

Electricity and gas

If you are unhappy with the size of your electricity or gas bill or have any other complaint about the service, contact your supplier first. An independent consumer body, energywatch*, was set up in November 2000 to represent the interests of all gas and electricity consumers. It provides advice and information to gas and electricity consumers, represents their views and is the first port of call for customers who have not been able to resolve complaints with gas or electricity companies.

The Office of Gas and Electricity Markets (OFGEM)* is the regulatory watchdog of electricity and gas companies. This independent body monitors energy suppliers and aims to ensure that they comply with their statutory obligations. In Northern Ireland, the watchdog is called the Office for the Regulation of Electricity and Gas (OFREG)*.

OFGEM aims to protect consumers' interests by ensuring they get genuine choice and value, and by promoting effective competition in both gas and electricity markets and regulating monopolies. It can also deal with issues passed on to it by energywatch which may involve the enforcement of any regulations against the energy companies.

OFGEM has set out guaranteed standards of performance for electricity and gas suppliers.

With electricity, you are entitled to fixed amounts of compensation for various delays (for example in giving customers notice of supply interruptions, dealing with company fuse failures, giving estimates of connection charges, and in dealing with meter problems, voltage complaints and charges and payment queries). So, if an engineer fails to keep an appointment, for instance, customers receive a fixed payment of £20. Payments are automatic for most of the standards and are normally made by reducing the customer's next electricity bill (though for delayed supply restoration and lack of notice of supply interruption, it is necessary to submit a claim).

Gas suppliers also promise to meet certain service standards. Failure to meet these standards again gives you fixed amounts of compensation. For example, with missed appointments, you receive compensation of £11 if British Gas or your supplier fails to turn up for an appointment, unless the supplier gave you 24 hours' notice that it could not keep the appointment.

There's also special treatment for older, disabled or chronically sick gas customers. British Gas maintains a Gas Care register and invites older, disabled or chronically sick customers to register for services including a free annual gas safety check. Similar services may be available from other suppliers.

Full details can be obtained free from your supplier.

Water

In England and Wales, the activities of every water company are regulated by the Office of Water Services (OFWAT)*, which is the economic regulator for the water industry. OFWAT is responsible for ensuring that water and sewerage companies in England and Wales provide their customers with a good-quality, efficient service at a fair price. WaterVoice (*www.watervoice.org.uk*) represents water customers in England and Wales. It decides what standards you can expect from your water company. There are ten regional committees of WaterVoice. However, the Water Act 2003 provides for the setting up of an independent Consumer Council for water. The regional WaterVoice Committees will be wound up.

As part of their licence each water company must have a code of practice that sets out what services are offered, gives details of charges, tells customers what to do in an emergency and lays down a procedure for making complaints. There are also codes of practice covering leakage. Leaflets explaining all these codes are available from your local water company: look under Water in the telephone directory or ask OFWAT. Since the passing of the Water Industry Act 1999, water disconnections have been banned. If you encounter difficulties paying your bills, ask your company about special assistance under the 'Vulnerable Groups' regulations.

Following the Water Act 1991 water companies are legally obliged to operate a Guaranteed Standards Scheme. Customers are entitled to claim a set amount, currently £20, every time there are unplanned interruptions of water supply lasting longer than 12 hours (unless the burst is on a strategic main), or if it takes longer to restore the water supply than the customer was told. You may also claim a refund of your sewerage bill each time your property suffers sewer flooding, subject to a limit of £1,000 per incident (limited to one per year).

If you cannot get satisfaction from the water company, write to the WaterVoice Committee for your area (the address is in the telephone directory under WaterVoice). If its intervention does not resolve the problem to your satisfaction, you can ask for your complaint to be passed to OFWAT's Director General.

In Scotland, write to the water authority for your area. If you are still not happy, write to the Water Industry Commissioner for Scotland*.

In Northern Ireland, contact the Water Services Office of the Department of the Environment*.

Unwholesome water

Water companies are under a legal obligation to maintain a supply of wholesome water, as laid down by the Water Act 1991. If yours does not, write to its head office, claiming compensation for any inconvenience you may have suffered.

Water meters

Since April 2000, you can request a water meter. The water supplier cannot force you to have a water meter installed unless your water usage is more than that for normal domestic use, for example if you have a swimming pool or regularly use a sprinkler. If your water company tells you that you must have a water meter installed, contact your local WaterVoice for advice. If you move to a house that already has a meter installed, you cannot get rid of it.

Communications

All communications – phones, faxes, Internet, television and radio – are covered by OFCOM, the Office of Communications★. OFCOM provides detailed advice and information about what you can expect from your phone company or Internet service provider. You can make a complaint to OFCOM if you think that a communications company has behaved badly.

Telephones

You have many rights as a telephone user. Some rights only cover you when dealing with BT or Kingston Communications in Hull; other rights cover all phone companies. Some of these rights are based on the Telecommunications Act 1984. Others come from European Union (EU) law. You also have all the rights that any other consumer has under general consumer law, such as the Sale of Goods Act 1979.

Rights cover areas such as the right to:

- a phone service
- an itemised bill
- be included in the phone book and directory enquiries, unless you prefer to be ex-directory
- a written contract for your phone service that includes at least:
  - the time it takes to connect the service at the start of your contract
  - the types of maintenance service offered
  - compensation or refund arrangements (or both) if the service is not met
  - a summary of the dispute resolution procedures
  - information on the level of service quality offered.

If you have a dispute with your phone company and you cannot reach an agreement you should contact the Office of the Telecommunications Ombudsman (OTELO)★ for advice. Most of the major phone companies are covered by the scheme.

Railways

The Strategic Rail Authority (SRA) was set up by the Transport Act 2000 to oversee the railways. Its responsibilities cover the three sectors of Passenger, Freight and Infrastructure, with the aim throughout being the creation of a 'Bigger, Better, Safer' Railway.

The SRA's key role is to promote and develop the rail network and encourage integration. As well as providing overall strategic direction for Britain's railways, the SRA has responsibility for consumer protection, administering freight grants and steering forward investment projects aimed at opening up bottlenecks and expanding network capacity. It is also responsible for letting and managing passenger rail franchises. On 15 July 2004 the government published its White Paper on the future of rail. The proposals include abolishing the SRA, with its responsibilities transferring to the Department of Transport.

Postal services

Broadly, the Post Office is legally responsible, in certain circumstances and within certain financial limits, for most things lost or damaged in the inland post. Responsibility to pay compensation only extends to paying compensation for an actual item lost or damaged (within the limits set by the Post Office). You have no right to financial compensation for anxiety, inconvenience or any further loss that is caused such as the value of any message or information or consequential loss.

If you are not satisfied with the way your complaint has been handled by the Post Office, say, you can get help and advice from Postwatch★, the new consumer watchdog for postal services. It was set up by the Postal Services Act 2000 to act as the 'voice of the consumer' in all *postal* matters. It aims to ensure that customers get the best possible service from post offices, Royal Mail and Parcelforce Worldwide. It acts independently of both the government and the Post Office.

The Postal Services Commission (Postcomm)★ is the economic regulator and it deals with licensing and price controls and competition. Its main duty is to ensure that a universal service is provided by Royal Mail.

Complaining to an electricity company about meter readings

Dear

[Reference: account number and bill]

Thank you for your letter of **[date]** concerning the above account.

I do not accept that the meter is recording accurately. The bill in question **[reference]** for **[£......]** reflects a greater than usual usage, but owing to **[circumstances: absence etc.]**, it should be less than usual.

I inspected the meter with all my electrical appliances turned off and noted that it continued to register **[......]** units of electricity consumption. It is clear that either the meter is faulty or that there is a leakage to earth, so the bill is not a true reflection of electricity used. I now wish to request you to carry out a test on the electricity meter at my home.

I look forward to hearing from you with a suitable date for the test to be carried out.

Yours sincerely

Asking OFGEM to intervene in a dispute with an electricity company

Dear

[Reference: account number and bill]

I am writing with reference to my dispute with the **[utility company]** which has yet to be settled to my satisfaction.

I am enclosing copies of all the recent bills and correspondence relating to the above account. As you will see, it appears that the meter is not recording correctly, because **[summarise argument]**.

I therefore wish you to intervene on my behalf. I understand that while you are considering the matter no legal action will be taken over non-payment of the bill, nor will my electricity supply be disconnected.

I look forward to hearing from you in due course.

Yours sincerely

encs.

Complaining to a gas company about a high bill

Dear

[Reference: account number]

I wish to complain about your bill dated **[date]** for **[amount]** which I received today.

This bill is unusually high, and I have reason to doubt its accuracy because **[details]**. I believe the gas meter in my home is defective.

Please check the bill again and arrange for an inspection of the meter at my home.

I look forward to hearing from you with a suitable date for the test to be carried out.

Yours sincerely

Asking energywatch to intervene in a dispute

Dear

[Reference: gas company and account number]

I am in dispute with the above supplier concerning my bill **[date; reference if any]** for **[£......]**.

I am enclosing copies of the relevant bills and correspondence relating to the above account. As you will see, I believe that the gas meter at my home is not working properly because **[details]** and I would like you to intervene on my behalf.

I look forward to hearing from you in due course.

Yours sincerely

encs.

Complaining to a gas company about defective servicing

Dear

[Reference: account number]

On **[date]** your engineer called to carry out a service of my gas central heating system **[details of system]**. Since then the system has exhibited defects: **[describe]**.

The Supply of Goods and Services Act 1982 requires you to carry out this servicing in a good and workmanlike manner, using that degree of skill and care reasonably to be expected from a firm purporting to be experienced in the work. The above defects show that you have failed to fulfil your legal obligations.

However, while reserving my rights, I am prepared to give you one last opportunity to undertake the necessary remedial work to bring the job up to a reasonable standard within a reasonable time.

If you do not carry out the remedial work within 14 days, I shall have no alternative but to retain another contractor to put the matter right and to look to you to bear the cost of the work, as I am legally entitled to do.

Yours sincerely

NOTE
If this does not resolve your problem, obtain three quotations from qualified Council for Registered Gas Installers (CORGI)* gas fitters, and send them to the supplier. If this does not resolve the matter, get the work put right by the gas fitter tendering the lowest estimate and send his bill to the supplier. If the supplier refuses to reimburse you for this, you can issue a claim in the county court.

Complaining to a water company about a break in water supply

Dear

[Reference: account number]

I am writing to confirm our telephone conversation of **[date]** to the effect that the supply of water to my home was interrupted for a period of **[......]** days from **[date]** to **[date]** inclusive.

Under the Water Act 1989, you are obliged to provide a supply of water that is sufficient for my domestic purposes. As you failed in this duty I am entitled to compensation for the loss and damage I suffered as a result, which were as follows: **[describe]**. I am enclosing copies of receipts for the necessary remedial work and reports from the repairers confirming that the damage arose from the insufficient supply of water.

As this interruption was unplanned, I am also legally entitled under the above Act to claim compensation of £20 for the first 24 hours and £10 for each additional 24 hours I was without water.

I look forward to receiving your proposals for compensation within 14 days of the date of this letter.

Yours sincerely

encs.

Asking OFWAT to intervene in a dispute with a water company

Dear

[Reference: water company and account number]

I am in dispute with the above company concerning the water supply to my home.

I enclose copies of the relevant correspondence. As you will see, on **[date]** the water supply to my home became unwholesome **[describe]**. This problem lasted for **[......]** days. I contacted the **[supplier]** on **[date]** to complain about this matter but the dispute has not been resolved to my satisfaction.

I understand that the water company is obliged under the Water Industry Act 1991 to maintain a supply of wholesome water and I therefore ask you to obtain for me the appropriate compensation for the inconvenience I have suffered. (If necessary, please refer my complaint to the appropriate department in the Drinking Water Inspectorate.)

I look forward to hearing from you in due course.

Yours sincerely

encs.

Complaining to a phone operator about a high telephone bill

Dear

[Reference: account number]

I am writing to you in connection with your bill relating to the above account, for **[£......]** covering **[period]**, which is unacceptably high and which does not reflect the use I have made of the telephone.

My reasons for disputing it are as follows: **[describe]**. As I believe the meter on my line must be faulty, I would like you to arrange to have it tested for accuracy as soon as possible.

I look forward to hearing from you with proposed dates for this testing.

Yours sincerely

Asking OFCOM to intervene in a dispute about a telephone bill

Dear

[Reference: number: bill date]

I am in dispute with **[phone operator]** about the above telephone bill, which is unacceptably high. My reasons for disputing the amount are as follows: **[describe]** and I am not satisfied with the phone operator's response to the effect that **[summarise]**.

I enclose copies of all relevant correspondence and bills and would ask you to intervene on my behalf.

I look forward to your response in due course.

Yours sincerely

encs.

Claiming compensation for inconvenience from British Telecom

Dear

[Reference: account number]

On **[date]** I reported to you that there was a fault on my telephone line **[telephone number]** whereby **[describe]**. I was told that the matter would be resolved by **[date]**. This did not prove to be the case and **[describe subsequent events]** meant that the fault was not remedied until **[date]**.

Under your Customer Service Guarantee, I am entitled to claim for compensation for inconvenience caused by interruptions of service, and I look forward to receiving your proposals for compensation within the next 14 days. If I do not hear from you within that period I will refer the matter to the Office of Communications.

Yours sincerely

Chapter 10

Finance

The whole system of regulating almost all those involved in selling and administering financial products and services was completely overhauled by the Financial Services and Markets Act 2000. In particular, the 2000 Act established a single focus for regulation, the Financial Services Authority (FSA)*, and a single complaints handling service, the Financial Ombudsman Service (see page 158). This chapter also focuses on banks, accountants and the protection given to consumers by the Consumer Credit Act 1974, which protects individual borrowers in a number of ways. In order to fall within the Act's jurisdiction, an agreement for credit must not exceed £25,000. Agreements to borrow money to buy land, and certain charge card agreements, such as those operated by American Express and Diners Club, are not covered.

Financial services

The FSA is the 'super regulator' providing a one-stop-shop for regulating most of those involved in financial services. Importantly, two of the FSA's statutory objectives are to protect consumers and to promote public understanding of financial services.

The FSA checks and authorises firms that offer financial services, such as banks, building societies, insurers and mortgage lenders. Requirements include honesty, competence and sound finances. Only firms that have FSA authorisation can offer financial products and services. Not covered by the FSA structure are loans, credit and debt and occupational pension schemes. Mortgages and general insurance have been included within the FSA's powers from 2004 and 2005.

The FSA sets the rules for complaints and compensation schemes; oversees the training of people providing financial services; and has the power to investigate and discipline firms breaking its rules. The FSA has also appointed a 'consumer panel', which advises the FSA on the implications for consumers of any new policies it develops.

Consumer information is provided through a consumer helpline (0845 606 1234), which you can ring if you have a financial complaint or problem and are unsure where to go for help. The FSA does not deal with the problem itself, though it can direct you to the Ombudsman.

The Ombudsman

Problems with financial services can often be resolved by taking up your complaint with the firm or provider direct, at branch or area level. If this does not resolve your problem, take your complaint further by writing to the head office of the firm concerned. Once you have followed any internal complaints-handling procedure the firm may have, it may be possible to refer your problem to the Ombudsman.

The Financial Ombudsman Service* was set up by the Financial Services and Markets Act 2000 to help settle consumer complaints about personal finance firms. It can help with most complaints about:

- banks
- credit cards
- endowment mortgages
- financial and investment advice
- insurance
- mortgages
- personal pension plans
- other personal finance products.

After a firm has looked at all aspects of your complaint, and sent a 'final response' letter, you can ask the Financial Ombudsman Service to help. The Service is free to consumers. Generally, its aim is to put you in the position you would be in if things had not gone wrong. This might include telling the firm to make good your losses. Decisions are binding on the firm, up to a total of £100,000.

However, the Financial Ombudsman Service does not deal with:

- personal loan and credit-card providers which are not banks or building societies
- general insurance brokers
- mortgage brokers
- firms' proper use of their 'commercial judgment' (for example, deciding whether to give someone a loan, what insurance premium to charge, or what surrender value or with-profits bonus to pay)
- the actions of someone else's insurance company (for example, after a car accident)
- the way an investment has performed.

You can get a complaint form by contacting the Financial Ombudsman Service and should send it in within six months of the date of the firm's final response.

The Financial Services Compensation Scheme

If an FSA-authorised firm has gone out of business, you may be able to get help from the Financial Services Compensation Scheme (FSCS)★. The Scheme pays compensation to consumers who have lost out through mis-selling or poor advice from an authorised firm which has ceased trading. The maximum compensation payable depends on the type of product involved, e.g. unit trust, life assurance and so on.

Credit

Being turned down for credit

No organisation is obliged to lend you money or give you credit, nor does it have to tell you why it will not do so, though you do have a legal right to see any information from a credit reference agency file on which lenders may have based their decision. However, there is nothing to stop you asking for your application to be reconsidered.

You have rights laid down by Sections 157–60 of the Consumer Credit Act 1974 which allow you to challenge the basis of a credit company's rejection of your application. If you write within 28 days of the notification of a credit refusal to the company which refused you credit, asking whether a credit reference agency has been used in considering your application, the company is obliged to tell you whether such an agency has been used and to give you its name and address. You can then write to the agency, requesting a copy of the file relating to your case. The agency is obliged to send you a copy of it for a fee, currently £2. If the information on the file is incorrect, you are entitled to have it amended or removed, and to receive notice within 28 days of pointing out the error that this has been done. Once the information has been corrected, you can re-apply for credit. However, a lender may not use a credit reference agency, but may instead use a point-scoring system. The process of scoring is generally automated whereby a computer allocates points to each answer to a series of questions. The total number of points determines whether you get credit.

Rebate on early settlement

Most consumer loan agreements are credit agreements regulated by the Consumer Credit Act 1974. Check the small print on your agreement; if the agreement is regulated by the Act, the small print will say so. This gives you two related rights:

(1) to pay off all amounts due at any time during the duration of the agreement, and
(2) to receive a rebate of the credit charges taking into account the earlier receipt of the money by the creditor.

In order to exercise the right of early settlement, you must send **written** notice to the creditor and pay off all you owe under the agreement, less any rebate allowable. Details of the various calculations governing the rebates allowed in the various types of loan agreement are set out in the Consumer Credit Regulations. The mathematics involved is complicated and is worked out by the credit company.

In order to help you exercise your right of early settlement, regulations under the Act say that the creditor is under a duty, once he has received written notice from the borrower, to supply you with a statement showing how much needs to be paid, and showing the basic calculations involved in arriving at that sum. This statement will not necessarily show all the details of that calculation. If a complete breakdown is required, request this in writing from the Office of Fair Trading (OFT)★.

If the creditor is considering your complaint, you can apply to the county court (sheriff court in Scotland) for the credit agreement to be reopened and the terms of the agreement to be rewritten. Take legal advice from a solicitor before applying to the court to have the agreement reopened and rewritten.

Extortionate credit

If your loan payments are exorbitant, or if the rate of interest you are being charged is very high, you are legally entitled to ask the creditor to reconsider the matter. Your right to do so is laid out in Sections 137–40 of the Consumer Credit Act 1974. You must convince the court that the loan is extortionate, and the court will assess how expensive the loan is in relation to the risk to the lender that the loan may not be repaid. Court action can be slow and expensive – if you would have difficulty in financing such action contact your local Citizens Advice Bureau (look in the phone book).

Credit-card rights

Paying by credit card (but not a charge card or a debit card) gives you the added protection of the Consumer Credit Act 1974, provided the goods cost over £100 and under £30,000. If you pay by this means, the credit-card company as well as the retailer is liable for any breach of contract. So you can claim for faulty goods against the retailer, the credit-card company or both. It is a myth that you have to go to the retailer before you can claim against your card issuer. We advise you to write to both parties when you are making your claim. You will not get two lots of compensation, but you will increase your chances of getting the problem sorted out.

You are also entitled to claim from the credit-card company if the retailer goes into liquidation. This cover is particularly useful if you have made a payment in advance, such as a deposit, to a company that subsequently closes down, for you would otherwise have to take your chances as an unsecured creditor. However, as a result of a recent court decision, you are not protected under s.75 for items you buy abroad.

Buying on hire purchase

If you buy something on hire purchase (HP), your contract is with the finance company, the lender, *not* the retailer who supplied the goods.

In such transactions, you have the same basic rights as if you had paid cash: it is implied in the credit agreement that the goods will correspond to any description given of them by the salesperson or in sales literature; will be of satisfactory quality; and, if you relied upon the retailer's judgement because you required the goods for a particular purpose, they should be reasonably fit for that purpose for which you acquired them. With hire purchase, these rights are laid down by the Supply of Goods (Implied Terms) Act 1973.

When it comes to rejecting faulty goods your rights last longer if you have bought on HP than if you have bought them for cash. If you are paying on HP, you have the common law right to reject faulty goods *throughout* the duration of the agreement. If you find a problem with the goods and want to reject them, stop paying the instalments, write to the HP company and state what the problem is – that the goods are unsatisfactory, for example, that you are rejecting them, and that they are available for collection by the company. If you reject the goods in this manner, the HP company must refund the payments you have made. There is a risk that if you stop your instalments the HP company will sue you. Although you will have a defence because the goods are faulty, you may not wish court proceedings to be started against you. Alternatively, rather than stopping your payments, tell the HP company that you are paying your instalments under protest until the matter is resolved.

If you do not want to reject the goods, but would like, for example, a free repair, you should write to the company, explaining what is wrong with the goods and that you would like a free repair.

You are also entitled to claim compensation for any expenses you incur which were reasonably foreseeable by both you and the company at the time you entered the HP agreement; for example, if you bought a car on HP and it proved faulty, the cost of alternative means of transport while the car was being repaired would be an allowable expense.

Once you have paid all the instalments on your goods, your consumer rights become the same as if you had paid cash.

New credit laws

A new consumer credit bill was introduced in Parliament in December 2004. It aims to enhance consumer rights by empowering consumers to challenge unfair lending. It will also drive out rogue traders and extend protection to all consumer credit agreements.

Banking

When you open a bank or building society account you are making a contract, and all the usual rules governing contracts to supply a service apply, including the stipulation that the bank or building society must carry out the contract with reasonable skill and care.

The banking code of practice was updated in 2003. The code aims to improve your rights and the service you are offered by banks and building societies. It includes provisions relating to the following:

- **fair conduct** – banks and building societies should always act 'fairly and reasonably' in dealings with customers
- **information on changes to your account** – you must be told of any changes to the terms and conditions, charges and interest rate of your account within specified time periods. If your savings and investment account is superseded by a new type of account, your account must either be kept at the same interest rate as a new account with similar features, or switched to another with similar features
- **plastic cards** – for any type of plastic card, credit card, bank card and so on, the maximum liability for money taken without your agreement is £50, or nil if the card is lost or stolen before it reaches you. You will lose this protection only if you've been 'grossly negligent' by, for example, writing your Personal Identification Number (PIN) on the card – and it is up to the bank or building society to prove that this is the case. Where you have never let the card out of your possession, and an unauthorised debt appears on your statement, you do not have to pay the first £50

- **confidentiality** – your personal financial details *won't* be passed to other companies in the banking group – such as their insurance or investment arm – without your consent. In practice, this probably means that new customers will be given a straight 'yes/no' choice of whether to give their consent, and existing customers (who are deemed to have agreed to this sharing of information) will be given the right to object
- **complaints** – all institutions must set up proper internal complaints procedures and tell you what these are.

For more information see *www.bankingcode.org.uk*

Unauthorised withdrawals

If a cashpoint withdrawal appears on your account statement which you suspect is due to a technical problem with the cash dispenser machine, write to your bank or building society. The bank will need to know whether you had your PIN written down, whether there is any possibility that another person (even a member of your family) may have borrowed your card and whether there is any chance that you had forgotten about a visit to a cash dispenser, since the date that appears on your statement is not always the same as the date when you withdrew the cash. If your branch is not prepared to settle the matter to your satisfaction, it is worth taking your claim to its head office and then to the Financial Ombudsman Service.

Since the banking code of practice came into force in 1992, subscribing banks have had to show that a withdrawal was made by the cardholder or someone authorised by the cardholder. If the bank insists that you made the withdrawal and that its technology is infallible, and will not make any sort of refund to you, you will need evidence to back up your claim that you did not withdraw the money. So make sure you can remember where you were at the time of the 'phantom' withdrawal and, if possible, try to prove that you had your card with you at the time. Statements from friends who were with you may help.

Direct debit problems

A standing order is an instruction you give to your bank or building society authorising it to pay a specific amount of money at regular intervals to another person or organisation. In other words, it is instructed to initiate payments from your account. You can pay by standing order to anyone who has a bank or building society account. If you want to change the amount of a standing order, you have to issue a new instruction to your bank to that effect.

With a direct debit, you give your bank or building society the authority to debit your account with payments requested by the payee with whom you agree payment terms by completing a direct debit form or 'mandate'; you instruct your bank or building society to permit a payee to draw on your account; the payee ('direct debit originator') initiates payment by asking your bank to release money from your account – your bank only allows the payee to draw on your funds.

Banks and building societies thus delegate responsibility for initiating payments to payees. Because control of the amount and timing of the payment is in the hands of the originator, every originator must be relied upon to operate the system properly. Unlike payees of a standing order, a payee can ask for payment by direct debit only if approved by the banks and building societies who run the direct debiting scheme.

Ultimately the banks and building societies guarantee that customers paying by direct debit do not suffer from originators' mistakes; they reimburse customers if a direct debit which does not conform to the customer's instructions is charged to the customer's account.

Stolen cheques

If your cheque book is stolen, you are not liable for any fraud provided you let your bank or building society know of the theft as soon as possible. But fraud using cheques that you have already written is another matter.

Unless you write out cheques using specific wording (see below), a thief can fake the signature of the person to whom you are paying the money (the 'payee') on the back of a cheque you have already written out, even if you have crossed it, pay it into his own account and, when it clears, withdraw the money and disappear. In these circumstances, you would have no redress against either the bank where the cheque was paid in or your own bank which paid the cheque. The problem is that virtually all cheques are transferrable. The two parallel lines simply mean that the cheque has to be paid through a bank account.

However, the Cheques Act 1992 states that if you write the words *'Account Payee'* or *'a/c payee'* with or without the word *'only'* on the face of a crossed cheque, you are protected against the cheque being transferred to a thief's account. If the bank where the cheque is paid in negligently credits an account other than that of the payee named on the face of the cheque, it will have to make good the payer's loss.

Accountants

Legally anyone can call themselves 'an accountant' but there can be a huge difference between the services offered by an unqualified person and those offered by a qualified professional. Chartered accountants, for example, undergo lengthy training and are required to maintain standards of professional conduct and competence supervised by the Institute of Chartered Accountants in England and Wales★ (or its sister bodies in Scotland and Ireland).

The range of services offered by accountants covers auditing, financial reporting, taxation, personal finance, corporate finance, financial management and information technology. To find a firm, first try personal recommendations. If you want a full list of chartered accountants practising in your area, contact the Institute. Draw up a shortlist and then ask whether they have experience in your field, what range of services they can offer, how fees are charged and so on.

When you instruct an accountant, you are entitled to have the work done with reasonable skill and care. This is laid down by the Supply of Goods and Services Act 1982. The accountant should also follow your instructions and any professional guidance and standards in the area. If giving investment advice, the accountant must comply with all the relevant rules and regulations under the Financial Services and Markets Act 2000.

The Institute will take up complaints against members and has a disciplinary procedure. Otherwise, you may have to go to court to get redress. This may be complex and expensive, so get legal advice before proceeding.

Rejecting a credit company's offer of a rebate on early settlement

Dear

[Reference: account number]

I am writing in response to your letter of **[date]** containing an offer of a rebate on the above credit agreement, taken out on **[date]**, which is regulated by the Consumer Credit Act 1974.

Under the Act, I have the right to pay off the outstanding debt at any time, having given notice to you of my intention to do so. I am legally entitled to a rebate on early settlement and, after giving notice, I am required to pay off the outstanding debt less the correctly calculated rebate.

As you are no doubt aware, the rebate is calculated by reference to a table set out in the Rebate in Early Settlement Regulations. In my particular case, I am entitled to a rebate of approximately **[£......]**. Your offer of **[£......]** falls short of the statutory amount and you are under a legal obligation to provide me with a further reduction in the debt.

If I do not receive your proposals for a further reduction within 14 days of the date of this letter, I shall have no alternative but to pursue the matter further.

Yours sincerely

Rejecting a credit company's demands for excessive increases in repayment

Dear

[Reference: account number]

I write in response to your letter of **[date]** informing me that the APR for my credit agreement has been increased from **[... per cent]** to **[...... per cent]**.

At the time of entering into the agreement, you assured me in full knowledge of my financial circumstances that although the APR was variable, it was unlikely that it would be increased beyond the **[...... per cent]** you were quoting. The above increase means that my monthly payments have now been increased from **[£......]** to **[£......]**.

The type of agreement that I have entered into with you is regulated by the Consumer Credit Act 1974. The fact that you have raised the APR on my agreement to an unacceptable level means that the agreement is extortionate as defined by the terms of Sections 137–40 of the Act.

I urge you to reconsider the unreasonable interest charge you have imposed and to reduce the APR to its original level or, alternatively, a reasonable level. If I do not receive your proposals for a reduction in the interest charge within 14 days, I shall have no alternative but to submit this matter to the adjudication of the county court without further reference to you.

Yours sincerely

Claiming a refund from a credit-card company on a purchase from a bankrupt supplier

Dear

[Reference: account number]

On **[date]** I ordered **[item]** from **[retailer]** at a cost of **[£......]** and for which I paid using my **[describe]** credit card. I have paid the relevant credit-card bill covering this purchase.

The **[item]** has not been delivered, despite letters to the supplier dated **[dates]** and I have discovered that the supplier has gone into liquidation.

I understand that under Section 75 of the Consumer Credit Act 1974 the credit-card company is liable to the customer for any breach of contract or misrepresentation along with the supplier of goods and services.

The **[supplier's]** failure to deliver the **[item]** is a breach of our contract, and as I paid by credit card I hold you liable for this breach. I therefore expect you to credit my account with the full purchase price of **[£......]** within the next 14 days. If you fail to reimburse me I shall have no alternative but to issue a claim against you in the county court for recovery of the money without further reference to you.

Yours sincerely

NOTE
If the credit-card company does not settle your claim, take it to court using the small claims track (see Chapter 17).

Querying erroneous charges on a credit-card statement

Dear

[Reference: account number]

I have received the current statement of this account, which contains charges for purchases that I have not made. The charge's reference is **[number]**, the supplier **[name]**, the amount **[£......]** and its date is **[date]**.

I have not made any purchases from this supplier. As I have neither lost my card nor revealed to anybody my card number, I believe that I am a victim of a credit-card fraud.

Please look into this matter without delay and send me copies of the voucher allegedly bearing my signature. If the purchase was made by telephone, please send me details of the transaction.

In the meantime, I am enclosing a cheque in respect of my outstanding bill less the sum of the disputed transaction. While this matter is being sorted out, I expect the disputed charge to be removed from my account, so that it does not incur interest.

I look forward to hearing from you within the next 14 days.

Yours sincerely

enc.

Asking a credit-card company to waive its fee

Dear

[Reference: account number]

I am currently reviewing my financial arrangements and am considering switching to one of the many credit cards with no annual fee and a lower interest rate.

I have been pleased with my card and would like to keep it if possible. However, there are now several cards with similar benefits (such as purchase protection insurance) to your card but cheaper.

If I am to stay with your company, I would therefore want you to waive the annual fee that I would otherwise be charged. If you are not prepared to do this, I shall have no alternative but to close my account with you and switch to another card issuer.

I would be grateful if you could let me know your position as soon as possible. I look forward to hearing from you.

Yours sincerely

Rejecting faulty goods bought on HP

Dear

[Reference: credit agreement number]

I acquired **[item]** on **[date]** from **[supplier]** under a hire-purchase agreement with you. The **[item]** has developed serious defects **[describe in detail]**.

In accordance with my rights under the Supply of Goods (Implied Terms) Act 1973, and my right to reject under common law, I now terminate my hire-purchase agreement with you on the grounds that the **[item]** was not of satisfactory quality when purchased.

I call on you to take back the **[item]**, and to refund all sums which I have paid to you under the agreement. These sums include the deposit and the instalments paid since the agreement was entered into, making a total paid of **[£......]**. In addition I am claiming compensation for the expenses, inconvenience and loss of use of the **[item]** due to the above defects.

In my view of the serious nature of the above defects, I am not prepared to consider any proposition that further attempts be made to repair the **[item]**, nor shall I be paying any further instalments.

I am therefore informing you that I am continuing to make my payments under protest.

Please let me know when you intend to collect the **[goods]** and to refund all the payments I have made.

Yours sincerely

Informing a bank's/building society's head office of unauthorised cashpoint withdrawals

Dear

[Reference: account number]

I am enclosing copies of my correspondence with your **[location]** branch, where my account is held.

As you will see, an unauthorised withdrawal has been made from my account from a **[details: type of dispenser, date, time]**. I could not have made this withdrawal because at the time I am supposed to have used the card I was elsewhere **[details]**. My Personal Identification Number (PIN) is not written down and I have not revealed it to anyone. Nor has my cashpoint card been lent to anyone.

I therefore maintain that these debits are not in any way the result of my actions, and are due to some defect in the procedure for processing cash card debits and withdrawals. Accordingly I expect to receive a revised statement within the next 14 days.

Yours sincerely

encs.

NOTE
If you do not receive a satisfactory response write to the Financial Ombudsman Service.

Complaining to a bank/building society about errors in the execution of a direct debit instruction

Dear

[Reference: account number(s)]

I have two accounts at your branch. One is in joint names **[specify account name and number]**; the above account is in my name alone.

There are no direct debits in respect of my account but a direct debit has been arranged in respect of the joint account. **[Details; payee.]**

Sums have been released from the wrong account, **[details]** resulting in an overdraft on the above account, for which I am now being charged.

On **[date]**, I was told that you were not liable for this and that it was the payee's responsibility to sort out the problem.

In order that I may clarify the situation, please let me have a copy of the direct debit instruction so that I may ascertain that all its details are correct.

I look forward to hearing from you within 14 days.

Yours sincerely

Rejecting a bank's/building society's denial of liability for the incorrect execution of a direct debit instruction

Dear

[Reference: account number]

Thank you for your letter of **[date]** enclosing a copy of the direct debit instruction made out in connection with **[payee]**.

The instruction was made out correctly, but you have made the following error in carrying it out **[details]**. Since the error is clearly yours I am not prepared to pay the relevant charges currently set against my account **[details]**.

I expect you to sort out the matter to my satisfaction within the next 14 days. If you do not, I shall take the matter up with the Ombudsman **[specify]**.

Yours sincerely

Requesting information on the use of a credit reference agency when an application for credit is rejected

Dear

[Reference: credit application number]

Thank you for your letter of **[date]** rejecting my application for credit **[details]**.

I cannot understand why my application has been turned down, and would like to know whether a credit reference agency has been used in considering my application. If this is the case, please give me its name and address so that, in accordance with my rights under the terms of Sections 157–60 of the Consumer Credit Act 1974, I may write to the agency concerned to ascertain whether the information it supplied to you is correct.

I look forward to hearing from you in due course.

Yours sincerely

Complaining about information supplied by a credit reference agency and asking for reconsideration of an application for credit

Dear

[Reference: credit application number]

I recently applied for your credit card under the above reference and my application was turned down. Your letter of **[date]** indicated that this was due to adverse information supplied to you by **[name]** credit reference agency.

I wrote to the agency to obtain a copy of my file and was surprised to find the following record **[describe]**. This matter has nothing to do with me. I therefore wrote to the agency again on **[date]** asking it to amend my file. The agency has agreed to do this.

In the circumstances, I would like you to reconsider my application, and look forward to hearing from you within the next 14 days.

Yours sincerely

Complaining to a bank about encashment of a stolen cheque

Dear

[Reference: account number]

On **[date]** I wrote a cheque **[number of cheque]** for **[amount]** payable to **[name]**, adding the word 'only' after the payee's name and the amount. I also crossed out the printed words 'or order' and wrote 'Account payee' between the two printed parallel lines.

The cheque was posted to **[payee's name]** on **[date]** but was intercepted by a thief who, I understand, wrote **[payee's name]** on the back of the cheque, so that it seemed that **[payee's name]** had authorised the transfer of the money to the thief. Having endorsed the cheque in this way, the thief paid it into his own account and, when it cleared, withdrew the money.

Since I made out the cheque to **[payee's name]** only and wrote 'Account payee' between the parallel lines, the cheque should have been paid into the payee's account only. In accordance with the Cheques Act 1992 the cheque was not transferable but was valid only between **[payee's name]** and myself.

As the cheque was not credited to the account of **[payee's name]** I am legally entitled to be reimbursed, and I therefore look forward to receiving your cheque for **[amount]** within seven days, or my account being credited with this sum.

Yours sincerely

Asking the Financial Ombudsman Service to intervene in a dispute with a bank

Dear

[Reference: bank/society and account number]

I am in dispute with the above **[bank/society]** in respect of unauthorised withdrawals made from my current account.

I am enclosing my complaint form and all the relevant correspondence, from which you will see that I have been unable to reach a settlement with **[branch]**, despite having contacted its head office.

I would therefore be grateful if you would consider the case on my behalf.

Yours sincerely

encs.

NOTE
This letter should accompany the form which will be sent on request if you phone the Financial Ombudsman Service.

Complaining about bad advice on an endowment mortgage

Dear

[Reference: endowment policy number and mortgage reference number]

I am writing to you to complain about the way I was sold my mortgage endowment policy.

I believe, for the reasons set out below, that I was mis-sold this policy and I am requesting you to investigate the sale. I am also requesting that you send me a copy of my endowment file so that I can see all the documentation you have relating to my case.

An adviser in your company sold me an **[name of policy]** endowment policy in **[date]**. The target amount was **[£......]**.

The reasons I am complaining are as follows: **[insert your reasons and any supporting information]**.

FSA rules require you to deal with this complaint. I therefore look forward to hearing from you within the next 14 days, with your proposals to resolve this matter.

Yours sincerely

Complaining about bad advice from a financial adviser

Dear

[Reference: product type and reference number]

I am writing to you to complain about the above product.

When I first talked to you on **[date]**, I made it clear that my circumstances were as follows **[describe]**.

I was led to believe that I was taking out a product that was appropriate to my needs. When I received **[document]** on **[date]** I discovered that the product did not meet my requirements as follows **[describe problems]**.

Under the Financial Services Authority's rules you are required to give consumers 'best advice', taking account of their personal details and circumstances.

The fact that the above product does not meet my requirements clearly shows that you have failed to give best advice. I therefore expect to receive compensation from you covering the difference between what I will get from the product and what I would have earned had you given best advice and advised me to take out a more appropriate product. I calculate this to be **[£......]**.

FSA rules require you to deal with this complaint. I therefore look forward to hearing from you within the next 14 days. If this matter is not resolved to my satisfaction, I will refer it to the Financial Ombudsman Service.

Yours sincerely

Asking the Financial Ombudsman Service to intervene in a dispute

Dear

[Reference: investment company and product number]

I am in dispute with the above investment company, which I understand is a member of your scheme.

I have been unable to reach a settlement with the company in respect of **[describe complaint]**. I am therefore referring the matter to you.

I enclose copies of my complaint form and all the relevant correspondence, and I look forward to hearing from you in due course.

Yours sincerely

encs.

NOTE
This letter should accompany the form which will be sent on request if you phone the Financial Ombudsman Service.

Asking the Financial Services Compensation Scheme (FSCS)* to compensate you

Dear

[Reference: investment company and product number]

I am in dispute with the above investment company, which I understand is authorised by the Financial Services Authority.

I have been unable to reach a settlement with the company in respect of **[describe complaint]**. I understand that the company has ceased trading **[give details of how you found out]**. I am therefore referring the matter to you.

I enclose copies of all the relevant correspondence, and I look forward to hearing from you in due course.

Yours sincerely

encs.

Complaining to an accountant about unsatisfactory work

Dear

I am writing to complain about the service you provided when I instructed you to prepare the following **[describe]**.

When I first spoke to you on **[date]** and showed you my files, I made it clear that my circumstances were as follows **[describe]**. It has now become apparent from **[source]** that the advice you gave me and the accounts you subsequently prepared on my behalf are deficient in the following respects **[describe]**.

The Supply of Goods and Services Act 1982 requires you to carry out your service as an accountant with reasonable skill and care. The problems described above show that you failed in your legal obligations. I therefore have a claim against you for breach of contract.

Because of your breach of contract I have suffered the following loss **[describe]**.

I consider that **[£......]** would be a reasonable sum of compensation for your failure to meet your legal obligations. I therefore look forward to receiving your cheque within the next 14 days.

Yours sincerely

Asking the Institute of Chartered Accountants to intervene in a dispute with an accountant

Dear

[Reference: name of firm of accountants]

I am in dispute with the above-named accountants concerning the service I received from the firm on **[date]**.

I enclose copies of the relevant correspondence. As you will see, the service I received from the firm caused me to suffer the following loss **[describe]**.

I contacted the accountants on **[date]** to complain about this matter but the dispute has not been resolved to my satisfaction.

Since the accountant involved is a Chartered Accountant, I am now referring the matter to you for investigation. I look forward to hearing from you in due course.

Yours sincerely

encs.

Chapter 11

Insurance

This section tells you how to claim on the main types of insurance policies held by consumers: home insurance (buildings and contents), holiday insurance and car insurance.

Claiming on your insurance policy

To make your claim, contact your insurance company (or broker, if you are insured with Lloyds) as soon as possible, stating your policy number and brief details of your claim. You will then get a claim form which you must complete and return, normally within 30 days.

On receipt of the claim, your insurance company may arrange for a loss adjuster to visit you to assess whether your claim is valid; it may pay the claim in full, or it may make an offer of less than the sum claimed.

Loss adjusters are independent of insurance companies and Lloyds' underwriters, and are hired to investigate and advise on claims on their behalf. You can in turn appoint a loss assessor who will charge a fee for representing you. The loss adjuster will ask you a number of questions to establish the validity of the claim and will then make a report to the insurer, which usually includes a settlement figure. If you are not satisfied by the insurance company's offer, write again explaining why you are dissatisfied.

If you have exhausted the insurance company's complaints procedure (set out in your insurance policy) and your claim has not been settled, contact the Financial Ombudsman Service★ (see page 158).

The Ombudsman deals with the unfair treatment of customers by insurance companies, poor service and maladministration. You usually have six months from the time you reach deadlock with the insurer in which to make a complaint. Awards recommended by the Ombudsman are binding on companies up to £100,000.

Claiming on buildings insurance

An insurance policy is not a maintenance contract. It is intended to provide cover for specific damage or loss – fire, storm or whatever – *not* to pay for your running repairs. It is a condition of buildings insurance that you keep your property in good condition and take reasonable steps to avoid damage to it.

If your insurance company is not prepared to settle your claim you will have to prove the validity of your claim. To succeed with a claim for storm damage, for example, you will have to prove that the property was damaged as a result of a violent wind accompanied by rain. You will need evidence backing your claim, so if you feel there is the slightest chance that your claim may be disputed, take photographs of the damage as soon after it occurred as possible and ask the repairer to give you a written report detailing the work that has been done to remedy the problem. You will also need evidence from the Meteorological Office★, for example, that there was a storm. If you do not provide this kind of evidence, it may be very difficult to prove your claim.

Claiming on contents insurance

Home contents insurance covers your household possessions, but only against certain eventualities such as theft. If your property has been stolen, you must report the theft to the police at once. If you do not, your insurance company could refuse to meet your claim. Check the wording of your policy to see how much to claim. If your policy offers 'new for old' cover, you are entitled to claim the cost of new items to replace those destroyed or stolen; with indemnity cover you claim the cost of replacing the item less an allowance for wear and tear.

Do not assume that your insurer is obliged to settle your claim by paying you cash. Many insurance companies reserve the right in their policies to repair or replace damaged or stolen items. If this is the case and you still opt for cash rather than replacement, the insurance company may reduce the amount payable to you by the value of a discount it would have obtained if you bought replacements from one of its chosen retailers.

If a thief broke into your house and damaged a door or smashed windows, for example, you could claim for the damage to the structure of the property on your buildings insurance. If the incident has damaged both the structure of your home and its contents and you have buildings and contents insured with the same insurer, you need only complete one claim form and the claim will be processed as one. If your buildings and contents insurance are with different insurers, you will have to make two separate claims.

If you are claiming for something that has been damaged but can be repaired – a scratched table, for example – claim the cost of repairs. You will need to get two or three estimates and then get the repairs carried out for the lowest price.

If you are dissatisfied by the insurance company's offer, try to get evidence, such as receipts and independent valuations, to back your claim.

Claiming on holiday insurance

Lots of things can go wrong with holidays, so it pays to take out comprehensive insurance when you book. The practice of travel agents making holiday discounts dependent on your buying their own travel insurance has been outlawed as anti-competitive. This leaves you free to shop around for the best deals. However, do not be tempted to forgo insurance altogether or to leave taking it out until you are due to depart – travel insurance should start from the time of booking your holiday just in case you have to cancel before you are due to depart. Read the terms of your policy carefully, and if you have to claim make sure you follow the procedures set out in it. Do not rely on a telephone call; make your claim in writing, and keep a copy.

The minimum cover you need will depend on your personal circumstances and your destination, but for a typical holiday you require the following:

- **medical expenses** – these should cover all reasonable medical, hospital and emergency dental treatment. The minimum cover should be about £250,000 in Europe; £1 million in the USA and the rest of the world

- **cancelling or curtailing your holiday** – the circumstances covered should include: the illness or death of the insured person, a close relative or business associate, or travelling companion; redundancy; jury service or being called as a witness in a court case; severe damage to the insured person's home by fire, flood or storm; and burglary or other criminal acts against him which necessitate his presence at home. The minimum cover should be the full cost of the holiday, including the deposit
- **belongings and money** – at least £1,500 cover should be provided for loss of, or damage to, the insured person's property and currency
- **delayed departure** – look for at least £20 or more after the first 12 hours' delay, and the full cost of the insured person's holiday if he cancels after the first full 24 hours' delay
- **delayed baggage** – if baggage is delayed by 12 hours or more on the outward journey the traveller will need cover to pay for emergency purchases until the baggage arrives. The minimum cover you should look for is £75
- **personal liability** – if the insured person accidentally injures someone or damages someone's property, he might be legally liable to pay compensation. Look for cover of £1 million.

If you have to claim you must get all the evidence before you return home, so keep all relevant receipts and bills. In the case of theft of an item you will usually be required to report the matter to the local police and get an incident report form from the police station. Take a copy of your policy with you on holiday so you know the exact extent of your cover.

If you have to cancel your holiday
Most holiday insurance policies cover cancellation and give details of the circumstances in which insurers will pay. Almost all policies cover those insured against inability to travel owing to illness or the illness of a close relative. Check the wording of your policy.

Reasonable care
Insurance companies may deny your claim if they consider you have failed to take reasonable care – for example, your claim may be denied on this basis if you leave valuable goods on the beach unattended when you go for a swim. Whether or not you took reasonable care will depend on the value of the goods and the

circumstances of the individual case. But it is always worth challenging an insurance company's refusal to pay if it is a member of the Financial Ombudsman Service.

Claiming on car insurance

You are obliged by law to have car insurance. The legal minimum you need covers claims made against you for personal injury to other people (including passengers) and their emergency medical expenses, damage to other people's property caused by you, and limited legal expenses. Most consumers want a more comprehensive policy than this and choose 'third party' cover. This gives the legal minimum cover extended to all public and private roads, plus cover for damage and injury to other people caused by your passengers. One step up from this is 'third party, fire and theft', which provides third party cover, plus cover in the event of your car and/or property fitted to it (such as the radio) being stolen or damaged by lightning, fire and explosion, or of the car being damaged during theft or attempted theft. This kind of cover does not include the contents of the car – a briefcase, sports bag etc. that might be in it. If you do not want to end up paying for your own repairs should your car be damaged, and you cannot prove that the damage was the other driver's fault, you need comprehensive insurance. This gives you the components of 'third party, fire and theft' cover, plus cover for damage to, and theft of, your car, and its contents (often up to £100), your medical expenses (often up to £100) and the cost of taking your car to a garage then home again after an accident.

Motorists often complain that the settlement offered by an insurance company is less than they feel the car is worth. Normally, the value of the car is taken as its market value at the time of the theft or damage being sustained.

If you are unhappy with the offer you receive, you will have to prove that the car is worth more than the sum offered. The sort of evidence that might help would be invoices for work or items which you consider must have enhanced the car's value.

If your car is written off following an accident but not totally destroyed, it may be possible to challenge the insurance company's offer by obtaining a report on the value of the car at the time of the accident from an independent assessor. The Institute of Automotive Engineer Assessors★ will give you the name of an assessor in your area. If you are a member of a motoring organisation such as the RAC or AA, ask that organisation to help with your claim.

Road accidents

If your vehicle is involved in an accident and you do not have comprehensive insurance, you will have to claim your losses from the driver of the other vehicle involved. Even if you are covered, you will usually have uninsured losses, such as any excess you have to pay on your own policy; loss of no-claims discount; compensation for personal injuries; loss of earnings; damaged clothes or other personal items; and the reasonable cost of alternative transport.

A no-claims discount is not a 'no blame' discount, so, even if the accident is not your fault, making a claim may affect your no-claims discount, or you may lose it altogether. In these circumstances you may prefer to pay for repairs yourself or come to an agreement with the other driver. But you must still notify your insurer about the accident. Send a letter to your insurer saying what has happened, making it clear that this is for information only and that you do not wish to make a claim.

You will be able to claim only if the collision was caused by the other driver's negligence – for example, because the other driver did not look where he was going. You would not be able to claim if no one was to blame for the collision.

With some comprehensive policies, your insurer will try to recover your uninsured losses on your behalf from the other driver. If you are trying to claim them back yourself, write to the other driver setting out the details of your claim. Although your legal rights to compensation are strictly speaking against the other driver, insurance companies will often step in, so you could find that you are dealing with the other driver's insurer.

Informing an insurance company of a claim on buildings insurance

Dear

[Reference: policy number]

I write to confirm our telephone conversation of **[date]**.

At **[time]** on **[date]** this property sustained serious damage **[describe]** due to **[circumstances]**. As it was an emergency I called in **[appropriate professional]**, who carried out temporary repairs. This work cost **[£......]**.

I wish to claim for the cost of the temporary repairs **[describe]** and for the eventual cost of remedying the damage as follows **[describe]**. Please send me the appropriate claim form.

Yours sincerely

Rejecting an insurance company's denial of liability

Dear

[Reference: policy number]

Thank you for your letter of **[date]**, in which you rejected my claim against the above policy for **[damage]** on the grounds that **[reason]**.

I refute your arguments on the basis of the wording of the policy, **[quote wording]**. Furthermore, I enclose a report from a relevant expert, backing up my claim as follows **[details of report]**.

This shows that the damage was caused by **[cause]** and was not in any way due to **[neglect etc.]** as you suggest. I am therefore covered by the terms of this policy, and expect you to reimburse me the sum of **[£......]**, as detailed in my original claim of **[date]**, within 14 days.

Yours sincerely

enc.

Rejecting an insurance company's continued denial of liability

Dear

[Reference: policy number]

Thank you for your letter of **[date]** rejecting my claim for **[£......]** following the damage to this property that occurred on **[date]**.

I maintain that the damage was caused by **[circumstances]** and should therefore be covered by the above policy. Prior to **[date of damage]** the property was well maintained and in good repair, as is proved by the enclosed **[proof – tradesmen's invoices etc.]**; therefore lack of proper maintenance could not have contributed to the damage.

I now ask you to reconsider my claim in light of this evidence, and look forward to receiving your cheque in settlement of my claim within 14 days.

Yours sincerely

encs.

Final letter to an insurance company in a dispute over buildings insurance

Dear

[Reference: policy number]

On **[date]** I claimed on this policy for **[describe damage]**, which occurred on **[date]**.

Although you have written to me on several occasions denying liability, I feel that I have presented sufficient evidence to you in the form of **[describe]** to prove that my claim is covered by the policy.

It is now **[......]** weeks/months since my claim was submitted and I feel that you have taken far too long to deal with this matter. Unless I receive your proposals for settlement within 14 days, I shall put the matter in the hands of the Financial Ombudsman Service.

Yours sincerely

NOTE
If your claim is not settled following this letter write to the Financial Ombudsman Service.

Rejecting an insurance company's offer on a claim

Dear

[Reference: policy number]

Thank you for your letter of **[date]**, offering only **[£......]** in respect of the **[item]** which was **[details of loss/damage]** on **[date]**.

Since receiving your offer I have found a valuation certificate made by **[valuer]** dated **[date]** valuing the **[item]** at **[£......]**. In the light of this valuation, a copy of which is enclosed, I feel that your offer is too low and ask you to reconsider my claim.

I look forward to receiving your revised offer within 14 days.

Yours sincerely

enc.

Informing an insurance company of a claim on holiday insurance

Dear

[Reference: policy number]

I wish to make a claim on the above holiday insurance policy.

I have just returned from holiday **[dates, location]**. On **[date]** my **[item]**, worth **[£......]**, was **[reason for claim: theft, damage etc.]**. I reported the matter to the police in **[place]** on the day of the occurrence and have written confirmation of this. Please send me the appropriate claim form.

I look forward to hearing from you in due course.

Yours sincerely

Informing an insurance company of a claim for a cancelled holiday

Dear

[Reference: policy number]

On **[date]** I booked a holiday **[describe: dates, location etc.]** with **[tour operator]**.

I am now unable to take this holiday because **[details of medical or other valid problem]**. As a result, I am left with no alternative but to cancel my holiday, and have therefore written to the tour operator to this effect.

In the circumstances I am making a claim on my travel insurance policy, which covers me for the full cost of the holiday in the event of cancellation or curtailment due to illness or injury.

I look forward to hearing from you in due course. If there is any other information that you need to process my claim please let me know.

Yours sincerely

NOTE
You may have to prove that the illness or other problem is serious enough to make you unable to travel. This will certainly involve getting medical or other evidence, so ask your GP or other professional to provide a report backing up your claim.

Rejecting an insurance company's offer following a claim on car insurance

Dear

[Reference: policy number]

Thank you for your letter of **[date]**, in which you offered me **[£......]** in respect of the damage **[describe]** to my vehicle **[make, model, engine capacity]** as a result of **[circumstances causing damage]** on **[date]**.

Since receiving your offer I have obtained an independent valuation of my car from **[organisation/garage]** to the effect that the market value of the car at the time of the above incident was **[£......]**. A copy of the report is enclosed.

In the light of this evidence I am not prepared to accept your offer, and I expect you to reconsider it, taking the above valuation into consideration. I look forward to hearing from you within 14 days.

Yours sincerely

enc.

Claiming compensation for damage to a vehicle caused by a negligent driver

Dear

[Reference: accident and registration numbers of both vehicles]

The collision which occurred between the above vehicles at **[time, date]** at **[location]** and which was caused, as you admitted, by your negligence and through no fault of my own, resulted in **[damage: describe]** to my vehicle.

I have made a claim for the above damage under my comprehensive insurance policy, but as a result of your negligence and your failure to notify your insurer of the accident I have incurred costs for uninsured losses **[details]** totalling **[£......]**.

I hold you directly responsible for these expenses and I am legally entitled to receive compensation from you. I therefore expect to receive your cheque for **[£......]** within 14 days.

Yours sincerely

NOTE
If the other driver does not reply to this letter or does not offer satisfactory compensation, send another letter threatening court action (see page 202).

Informing your insurer that you have had an accident but you do not wish to make a claim

Dear

[Reference: accident and registration number of your vehicle]

For information only

I am writing to advise you that I was involved in an accident with another vehicle on **[date]**. The details are **[describe nature of accident]**.

My car suffered the following damage **[details]**. The other driver has admitted liability and agreed to pay for repairs.

Therefore the purpose of this letter is purely to notify you of the accident. I do not wish to make a claim on my insurance policy.

Please acknowledge receipt of my letter within 14 days.

Yours sincerely

Threatening a negligent driver with court action

Dear

[Reference: accident and registration number of both vehicles]

I have not received a reply to my letter of **[date]** and now write to inform you that, unless I receive your satisfactory proposals for settlement of my outstanding claim within seven days of the date of this letter, I shall have no alternative but to issue a claim against you in the county court for recovery of the money without further reference to you.

Yours sincerely

Asking the Financial Ombudsman Service to intervene in a dispute with an insurance company

Dear

[Reference: insurance company and policy number]

I am in dispute with the above insurance company, which I understand is a member of your scheme.

I have been unable to reach a settlement with the insurance company in respect of an offer it made in connection with **[item]** following my claim of **[date]**. I am therefore referring the matter to you for investigation.

I enclose copies of all the relevant correspondence, and look forward to hearing from you in due course.

Yours sincerely

encs.

Chapter 12

Solicitors

Whenever you instruct a solicitor to act on your behalf, you are making a contract. The contract has certain terms, the most obvious of which are that the solicitor will do the work – the conveyancing of your house, say – and that you will pay for that work.

What to ask a solicitor

- **How much do you charge?** Solicitors charge for their services generally on an hourly rate. Rates can vary as there is no uniform way of calculating them. Solicitors' charges are based on factors like the type of work being done, the solicitors' expertise and experience, the speed at which you need advice and where the firm is based. Find out the firm's hourly rate before you seek legal advice from it. Solicitors are now free to advertise their rates, but few choose to do so.
- **How many hours' work are likely to be involved?** Get a written estimate and set a ceiling on the costs.
- **What other costs might be involved?** It may be necessary to use a barrister or to get expert evidence.
- **When will I have to pay?** Get a clear timetable of payment.
- **What are you going to do next and what is the timescale involved?**
- **Would you confirm the advice given in writing? And what do I need to do next?**

Solicitors' code of conduct

The Solicitors' Costs Information and Client Care Code aims to ensure clients are given all the relevant information, in particular the costs of the legal services, at the outset and during the progression of the case, the details of the person responsible within the firm for dealing with the case, and details of the firm's complaints handling system, which all firms are required to have.

Under the code, costs information must not be inaccurate or misleading and must be clear to a layman. Also, the solicitor should advise how costs are calculated, so if the firm charges at an hourly rate, the rates should be set out. Where possible the solicitor should give an estimate of costs and explain if it is possible for you to fix an upper limit beyond which the solicitor must seek authority to continue with the work. In contentious matters (where court proceedings have been started) the solicitor should explain your potential liability for paying your own costs and those of the other party.

All the above information can be included in a letter given to you at your initial meeting with your solicitor. This letter is called a 'client care letter' or a letter of appointment. Alternatively, the solicitor may choose to give you a copy of the firm's written terms of business.

You should also be informed about the status of the person handling your case. If you are told that a solicitor will be dealing with your case, you are entitled to assume that the case will not be handled by a trainee solicitor, a legal executive or a paralegal.

Conditional fees

Solicitors and barristers often take on consumer cases on a 'no win, no fee' basis where the solicitor gets no fee if the case is lost and will write off the time spent working on the case. However, if you win the case your solicitor gets the usual fee plus an extra amount which will be a percentage of the normal fee up to a maximum of 100 per cent. The fee arrangement must be agreed in writing in advance. Also, because so many cases settle by negotiation without going to court, the agreement must spell out what constitutes a 'win'.

Usually you will pay an insurance premium to cover the other side's costs and your expenses if you lose. If the solicitor you use is part of the Accident Line★ scheme endorsed by the Law Society, you can pay a one-off fee for insurance cover in personal injury cases. The Law Society★ has details of cover for other types of dispute. For further information, see 'No win, no fee' actions, a free leaflet published by the Community Legal Service Direct★.

The final reckoning

Unfortunately the final bill may be much more than the original estimate. It is risky taking a case to court – even if you win, you may have to pay some of your own fees. You may have to accept less than you claimed because of the risks involved in proceeding after an offer has been made. And if you lose, you might have to pay the other side's costs as well. All these factors should be considered when contemplating whether to use a solicitor.

It is not possible to calculate a solicitor's fees exactly as there is no set scale of charges. However, it is implied into the contract between both parties that the solicitor's bill must be fair and reasonable.

If you are unhappy with the bill you receive for 'contentious work' (that is, where court proceedings have been started), you should request a detailed breakdown of the bill. The solicitor is obliged to provide you with this under Section 64 of the Solicitors Act 1974. To challenge the bill further, you can apply for the costs to be 'taxed' in court. This means that a special bill is drawn up and the court decides whether each item is fair and reasonable.

A word of warning – 'taxation' as defined above can be expensive. Not only will you have to pay a fee to the court to have the bill taxed, but, if the bill is reduced by less than one-fifth, you will lose the court fee and have to pay the solicitor's costs of going to court as well as your own.

If you feel that a bill for 'non-contentious work' (where the case being handled by the solicitor does not involve court proceedings) is too high, ask the solicitor involved for a detailed breakdown of the charges. If, having received a detailed breakdown, you still feel the bill is too high, ask the solicitor to apply to the Law Society★ for a Remuneration Certificate. This states whether the solicitor's bill is fair and reasonable and, if it is not, suggests another reasonable sum. If you have not paid your bill, your solicitor is entitled to ask you to pay half of the fees, plus VAT, and disbursements. If you feel that the certified amount is still too high, you still have the right to apply for the costs to be assessed by the court. You can call the helpline operated by the Law Society's Consumer Complaints Service (CCS)★ with queries about Remuneration Certificates.

The procedure for complaints about solicitors' charges in Scotland is broadly similar to that in England and Wales. However, there is no statutory right to a detailed breakdown of the bill and system of Remuneration Certificates. So regardless of court proceedings, if you wish to challenge a solicitor's bill, you must require him to have it taxed. This is done by the Auditor of Court. Otherwise complain to the Law Society of Scotland* arguing that overcharging amounts to incompetent work (see below).

Incompetent work

If you have a complaint about the way your solicitor is handling your case, you should first try to resolve the problem with the firm. Under professional practice rules solicitors must have a procedure for handling complaints. Your solicitor should have told you, when you first instructed the firm, whom to contact with a complaint. If you have not been given a name, write to the Complaints Handling Partner.

If you believe that your solicitor's work is incompetent or you have received poor service, you can complain to the CCS. The range of problems the CCS investigates includes delay in answering your letters or failing to answer them at all; delay in dealing with your case; failing to deal with your money properly; deception; failing to hand over your papers at your request when you are not in debt to the solicitor; and any substandard work which may have caused you inconvenience or distress, but has not caused you a financial loss for which you could sue.

Once you have complained to the CCS, it will investigate your claim and contact the solicitor on your behalf in an effort to resolve the problems you are experiencing. If appropriate, the CCS can take disciplinary action against the solicitor. The CCS also has powers to award compensation of up to £5,000. The Law Society of Scotland has broadly similar powers.

In addition, the Legal Services Ombudsman* oversees the way in which complaints against solicitors (and barristers and licensed conveyancers) are handled by the appropriate professional bodies. Before you contact the Ombudsman you must have exhausted the complaints procedure of the CCS. If you have done so, and are not satisfied with the handling of your complaint or the decision reached, you can then ask the Ombudsman to investigate on your behalf. There is no limit on the amount of compensation that may be awarded by the Ombudsman, but awards are not strictly binding. You must complain within three months. In Scotland, you should contact the Scottish Legal Services Ombudsman*.

Claiming for negligence

If you claim that your solicitor has been negligent, and you want financial compensation, you may have to take the claim to court. Get advice on your legal position from another solicitor, preferably one with experience of negligence work. If you cannot find an appropriate solicitor to help you, the CCS may put you in touch with a member of the Negligence Panel of the Law Society*, who will give you up to an hour's free advice. If you decide to proceed, you can ask that solicitor to take on your case. In Scotland, if you cannot find a solicitor to act for you, the Law Society of Scotland will appoint a solicitor (called a 'troubleshooter').

In England and Wales, if your claim does not exceed £5,000 your case would normally be dealt with under the small claims track in the county court. If you want to claim more than this, your claim will be referred to the fast track (claims up to £15,000) or the multi track (claims over £15,000). In both cases you should seek the advice of a solicitor. In Scotland, claims up to £750 are heard under the small claims procedure of the sheriff court. Claims over £750 but under £1,500 are heard under the summary procedure. (See also page 298).

Changes to the regulation of legal services

At the time of writing, Sir David Clementi had delivered his final report on the regulation of legal services, which proposes some wide-ranging changes.

The Clementi report recommends setting up a legal services board which will be responsible for ensuring that solicitors and barristers are properly regulated by their professional bodies.

There are also proposals for an independent complaints-handling service which will operate as a single gateway designed to provide better access for consumers who wish to complain about a legal service.

For more information see *www.legal-services-review.org.uk*.

Asking a solicitor for a breakdown of a bill

Dear

[Reference: invoice number]

Thank you for your letter of **[date]** containing your invoice for **[£......]**.

As you know, we have not been able to reach agreement on the sum that I should pay you for the **[service]** you did on my behalf.

So that I can get a clearer understanding of the component parts of your bill, I would be grateful if you would provide me with a detailed breakdown of all the items involved. I am entitled to this under Section 64 of the Solicitors Act 1974.

I look forward to hearing from you within 14 days.

Yours sincerely

Asking a solicitor to obtain a Law Society Remuneration Certificate

Dear

[Reference: invoice number]

Thank you for your letter of **[date]** containing a detailed breakdown of the work undertaken on my behalf and the costs accruing to it.

I am still not satisfied with the amount that I am expected to pay for the **[service]** undertaken on my behalf.

I am legally entitled to instruct you to obtain from the Remuneration Certificate department of the Law Society a Remuneration Certificate stating what, in the Society's opinion, is a fair and reasonable charge for the work done. I would be grateful if you would now do so.

I look forward to hearing from you within 14 days.

Yours sincerely

Paying under protest while a solicitor obtains a Remuneration Certificate

Dear

[Reference: invoice number]

On **[date]** I asked you to apply to the Law Society for a Remuneration Certificate.

I am concerned that if your account remains unpaid you will charge me interest. To avoid that eventuality, I enclose a cheque for the full amount of your bill. This payment is made on the strict understanding that it is subject to the outstanding application for a Remuneration Certificate continuing and that I will be appropriately reimbursed should the Certificate state that your bill should have been lower. If you do not agree to this condition, please return my cheque.

Yours sincerely

enc.

NOTE
Solicitors do have the right to charge interest on unpaid bills, hence the need to pay under protest to avoid subsequent interest charges on whatever fee is finally agreed upon.

Complaining about the slowness of a solicitor's conveyancing

Dear

[Reference: account number or similar]

As you know, on **[date]**, I instructed you to undertake certain conveyancing work on my behalf. I am becoming increasingly concerned about the amount of time you are taking to complete the work. I would therefore be grateful if you would clarify in writing the following points:

(a) why the matter has taken so long to get to its current stage

(b) what is left to be done and how long it should take

(c) your estimate of the costs incurred so far.

I look forward to hearing from you by return.

Yours sincerely

Asking the CCS to intervene in a dispute with a solicitor

Dear

[Reference: name of solicitor]

I would be grateful if you would consider my complaint about shoddy work by the above-mentioned firm of solicitors, whom I instructed on **[date]** to perform **[service]** on my behalf.

I enclose copies of all the relevant correspondence together with my own diary of events relating to the problem. The gist of my complaint is that the above solicitor's work has proved substandard in the following way: **[problem in detail]**. I understand that you may send copies of these documents to the solicitor concerned. If you require any further information, please contact me.

I look forward to hearing from you in due course.

Yours sincerely

encs.

Complaining to the Ombudsman about the Consumer Complaints Service (CCS)'s handling of your claim

Dear

[Reference: name and address of solicitors]

I am writing to you about my dispute with the above firm of solicitors in respect of **[describe]**.

On **[date]** I sent my file of papers to the Law Society's Consumer Complaints Service (CCS) and asked it to intervene. On **[date]** the CCS contacted me saying that it was unable to resolve my complaint to my satisfaction for the following reasons **[describe]**.

I do not regard the CCS's response as satisfactory because **[describe]**. I am therefore referring the matter to you for investigation.

I enclose copies of all the relevant papers, and I look forward to hearing from you in due course.

Yours sincerely

encs.

Chapter 13

Health

NHS

The NHS is a bewilderingly large organisation, so it can be difficult to know where to turn if you experience problems. Your local Independent Complaints Advisory Service (ICAS) can provide free help about how to complain about NHS services. ICAS works closely with your Patient Advice and Liaison Service (PALS) in England and Wales (Local Health Council in Scotland, Health and Social Services Council in Northern Ireland).

Before taking action, and at any time during the investigation, you can seek help and advice from ICAS.

All NHS trusts, GPs, dentists, opticians and pharmacists are covered by a complaints procedure. There are set time limits within which you must complain and receive a response, and if your complaint is not resolved satisfactorily at a local level an independent review panel should investigate it.

If you have a complaint about the services or treatment you receive from the NHS – whether it is from a hospital, GP, nurse, optician, pharmacist, dentist or walk-in centre – and you want an apology and explanation – you should refer the matter directly to the person involved. This procedure is known as local resolution and it should be possible to resolve the problem in this way. Talk to the doctor, nurse or whoever else is involved about what happened and explain what you would like done about it. If you would prefer to talk to someone who was not directly involved in your care, write to the complaints manager at the Primary Care Trust. The address will be in the phone book. In most surgeries, the practice manager will also take on the role of complaints manager.

You have to make your complaint within one year of the problem coming to your notice. If you complain about a GP then the complaints manager in the health authority may investigate. They may need to look at your medical records and meet you to gather the facts. You can expect to get an acknowledgement of your complaint within two days and a full written response within ten working days.

If you are not satisfied with the response, you can request an independent review by an independent review panel, but this must be done within 28 calendar days of the written reply to your complaint. The response should tell you who to contact. Your request will be considered by a specially trained member of the trust or health authority – the convener – who will ask you to explain in writing exactly why you are still dissatisfied. The convener will decide within ten working days whether or not to set up an independent review panel. Note that although you have the right to request an independent review, you do not have an automatic right to have one carried out. If a review panel is set up, they will write to you to tell you which matters the panel will investigate. The panel will fully re-examine your complaint and a final report will be sent to you and the other people involved. The chief executive of the trust or health authority will write to inform you of any action to be taken.

If your request is turned down, you should be informed of your right to appeal to the Ombudsman (see below). You can phone NHS Direct on (0845) 4647 (or (0845) 424 2424 in Scotland), which can put you in touch with someone who can help you make your complaint, if necessary.

If you are still dissatisfied after the NHS complaints procedure has been completed you can ask the Health Service Ombudsman★ to investigate your case. The Ombudsman is independent of the NHS and the government, and his services are free. As well as complaints about NHS services, he can investigate complaints about how the complaints procedure is working if, for example, you want to appeal against a refusal to set up an independent review panel. You must appeal to the Ombudsman in writing within a year of the event. If the Ombudsman decides to take on your case, he will undertake a thorough investigation and make recommendations to the relevant NHS bodies. He will often refer the case back to the convener for reconsideration. The Ombudsman will not generally take on a case which has not first been through the NHS complaints procedure, or a case which is being dealt with by the courts. If you have any doubt as to whether the Ombudsman can deal with your complaint, contact his office beforehand. The Health Service Ombudsman cannot award compensation, but can ask the NHS authority or trust to remedy or compensate for any injustice or hardship suffered.

If you think an NHS professional has behaved unethically or unprofessionally (e.g. drunkenness or indecency) you can complain to the professional body with which he is registered: the General Medical Council (GMC)★ for doctors, the General Dental Council (GDC)★ or the General Optical Council (GOC)★. If your complaint is about a nurse, health visitor or midwife, contact the United Kingdom Central Council for Nursing, Midwifery and Health Visiting (UKCC)★.

Finally, if you want to claim financial compensation you will prob- ably need to take legal action and prove negligence in court. It is vital in these circumstances to get advice from a solicitor who specialises in this area. Action for Victims of Medical Accidents (AVMA)★ (a national charity) can put you in touch with a solicitor and support groups.

Your Guide to the NHS

What you can expect from the NHS, and what you can expect in the future as improvements to health services are made, are set out in *Your Guide to the NHS*. This covers all aspects of NHS care, including hospital, community health, dental, optical, pharmaceu- tical and ambulance services.

The guide includes core principles that aim to set out what you can expect from the NHS, including the principles that the NHS will:

- provide a universal service for all, based on clinical need, not ability to pay
- respect the confidentiality of individual patients and provide open access to information about services, treatment and perfor- mance
- shape services around the needs and preferences of individual patients, their families and their carers
- provide a comprehensive range of services
- respond to different needs of different populations

- work continuously to improve quality services and to minimise errors
- work together with others to ensure a seamless service for patients
- keep people healthy and work to reduce health inequalities
- devote public funds for healthcare solely to NHS patients.

In addition there are national standards of care setting out commitments on performance relating to particular conditions, for example: cancer, mental health and coronary heart disease.

What to expect from GPs

Your Guide to the NHS says that:

- your practice nurse or GP will explain what is wrong with you, the best treatment for your condition and the likely outcome
- if your GP needs to refer you to hospital, you will be told why you are being referred, and what will happen when you go to hospital
- your GP must make sure that all patients have access to appropriate general medical care 24 hours a day.

GPs should have a practice leaflet, telling you when the surgery is open, how to make an appointment for a consultation and the arrangements for getting advice over the phone and for home visits. Leaflets should also tell you how to contact your GP outside normal surgery hours, for example, and how to order a repeat prescription.

In addition:

- you will be able to see a health professional (such as a practice nurse) within 24 hours, and have a GP appointment within 48 hours
- people with chronic conditions will be able to pick up a repeat supply of their medicines from their pharmacist, without having to go back to their GP each time
- you may be treated in a GP practice instead of having to travel to hospital for treatment.

What to expect from hospitals

If you need hospital treatment, arrangements are usually made by your GP, dentist or optician. You should be given regular information about how long you will have to wait:

- for an outpatient appointment, you can expect to wait no more than 26 weeks
- at the outpatient clinic you should be seen within 30 minutes of your appointment time
- for admission as an inpatient you can expect to wait no more than 18 months
- if your GP or dentist refers you urgently with suspected cancer, you will be seen by a specialist within two weeks
- if you are suffering from chest pain for the first time and your GP thinks this might be due to angina, you should be seen by a specialist chest pain clinic within 2 weeks.

When it is time for you to be admitted, your hospital will either write to you with your appointment date, time and directions to your clinic, or it may ask you to phone the staff to make an appointment on a suitable date.

After you are admitted, your nurse or doctor should explain what is wrong with you, and discuss the different treatments for your condition, and the risks and benefits of each treatment. If you decide to go ahead with treatment, you may be asked to sign a consent form, after you have been given a full explanation of what is proposed.

Hospitals should keep any relative or friend you name informed about your condition. You can see your records if you ask. Your participation in medical research or medical student training can only take place with your agreement.

NHS staff are obliged to respect your privacy and dignity.

Medical records

The Access to Health Records Act 1990 entitles you to see your paper medical records written on or after 1 November 1991. To do so, send a written request to the holder of the record (your GP or dentist, for example), or, in the case of hospital records, the local health authority (health board in Scotland and Northern Ireland). The holder must give you access to your records within 40 days; you can choose either to go to see the records or be sent a copy.

You get access free if your records have been added to in the last 40 days (in practice, if you have been treated during this time). If your records have not been amended recently, you can be charged up to £10. If you think the record is incorrect, you will have to ask for it to be put right. If the holder disagrees with you, a note of your views must be put on your file.

Remember, though, that you have no right of access to information recorded before the start date of 1 November 1991. The only way you will be able to see previously recorded paper records is if the holder of the records – your GP, for example – is willing to show you on an informal basis.

You also have a right under the Data Protection Act 1998 to see any electronically held records. You need to make a written request to the holder of the records, who may make a charge of up to £10 for each register entry, although in some cases the information will be provided free of charge. When writing you must state that you are requesting information under Section 7 of the Data Protection Act 1998. You should get a response within 40 days. If not you should complain to the Information Commissioner* who can enforce your right to know.

Private care

For most, the choice to go private rather than NHS is based on much more than just having your own room and a nice menu to choose from. The main benefit of private health care is that it offers you choice. However, this freedom of choice does not necessarily equate to superior clinical care, nor does it give you increased or enhanced legal protection.

Research by *Health Which?* has shown that most independent hospitals are much smaller than their NHS equivalents, so intensive-care facilities can be limited to just a small number of beds. As private hospitals do not provide accident and emergency services, there will not necessarily be an anaesthetist around to deal with emergencies 24 hours a day. In fact, an independent hospital may have just a single doctor on the premises at night. However, if you receive private treatment in a private wing of an NHS hospital, and something does go wrong, you are more likely to get immediate access to emergency facilities.

Access to redress in independent hospitals is more limited than in NHS hospitals. Unlike the NHS, there is no industry-wide statutory complaints system or independent ombudsman.

The Healthcare Commission* is responsible for regulating independent hospitals. The NCSC requires all independent hospitals to have a complaints procedure and it will investigate any complaints arising from a breach of its regulations.

Legally speaking, independent hospitals are responsible for problems resulting from the premises, equipment or its employees, such as nurses and administrators. Hospitals are also required to give patients full written details of the cost of their treatment, and any terms and conditions that apply.

While independent hospitals should now investigate any complaints about consultants working on their premises, they are not legally responsible for problems arising from the clinical care administered by consultants, who usually work in independent hospitals on a sub-contracted basis. Therefore, if your complaint is not resolved satisfactorily, your only option is to sue your consultant.

And, although each hospital must now have its own complaints procedure, patients still have no recourse to an ombudsman (though this may change).

If there is a problem with your treatment that amounts to 'serious professional misconduct', you can complain to the General Medical Council (GMC)* or, if the hospital is in England and a member, you can complain to the English Community Care Association*, both of which have their own complaints procedure.

Complementary medicine

These therapies are not usually taught in medical school. Anyone can set up as a complementary practitioner or therapist, although osteopathy and chiropractic are now regulated by legal statute. This means that all osteopaths and chiropractors must be members of the General Osteopathic Council* or the British Chiropractic Association* in order to practise.

If you want advice on finding practitioners of other complementary therapies contact the British Complementary Medicine Association* or the Institute for Complementary Medicine*.

Complaining to your local practice about a doctor's conduct

Dear

[Reference: doctor's name and practice]

I wish to complain about the quality of service I have received from the above GP.

At **[time]** on **[date]** I telephoned the surgery and asked them to send a GP as quickly as possible for the following reason **[describe]**. However, the doctor's behaviour was unsatisfactory in the following way **[describe]**. I was dissatisfied with his diagnosis and undertook to organise **[the patient's]** admittance to hospital **[name]**, where he was diagnosed as **[describe]** by **[second doctor]**. The **[patient]** was subsequently given treatment for this condition **[describe]**. The behaviour of **[initial doctor]** was unacceptable and I would be grateful if you would investigate his conduct.

I look forward to hearing from you in due course.

Yours sincerely

Requesting an independent review

Dear

I am writing further to the letter of **[date]**, which I received from my **[doctor's surgery/local health authority/local NHS trust]** concerning my complaint about **[doctor]**.

They have investigated my complaint but I am not satisfied with their response. I consider that my complaint is very serious. It is clear to me that the doctor was in breach of **[his/her]** professional terms of service in that **[describe nature of events]**. I therefore wish to pursue my complaint further.

I understand that you have been appointed as the convener in this case, and would be grateful if you would consider my request for an independent review panel to be convened to investigate my complaint.

I look forward to hearing from you in due course.

Yours sincerely

Complaining to your Health Authority about a dentist's charges

Dear

[Reference: dentist's name and address of practice]

I am writing to you to complain about the above dentist's charges.

On **[date]** I visited his surgery for the first time. After an examination he told me I needed **[describe treatment]** and I agreed to have National Health treatment. When this was completed I was presented with a bill for **[£......]**, a copy of which is enclosed. This was unacceptably high.

When I questioned it, **[dentist]** told me his reasons **[describe]** which I found unacceptable, and so I refused to pay the bill. Subsequent events **[describe]** left me no alternative but to pay the bill in full under protest.

I am dissatisfied with the outcome of this matter and I would ask you to look into it on my behalf.

I look forward to hearing from you in due course.

Yours sincerely

Complaining to the General Dental Council about a dentist's behaviour

Dear

[Reference: dentist's name and address of practice]

I wish to complain about the behaviour of the above dentist.

When I attended his surgery at **[time]** on **[date]**, his behaviour was unprofessional **[describe]**. As a consequence of this behaviour, I felt unable to go through with the appointment and promptly left the surgery.

I would therefore be grateful if you would investigate the conduct of **[dentist]**.

Yours sincerely

Complaining to an optician about unacceptable service

Dear

[Reference: make and model of spectacles]

On **[date]** I attended an appointment for an eye test. You then prescribed lenses, and I selected suitable frames.

When I collected the spectacles I complained that the lenses were not consistent with those selected as a result of my eye test **[describe problem]**. Despite your assurances to the contrary, the problem persisted. I subsequently visited your shop on **[date]** but was told that you were not prepared to replace the spectacles, nor were you prepared to adjust them.

The Supply of Goods and Services Act 1982 requires you to carry out your services with reasonable skill and care. It also requires you to use materials of satisfactory quality and reasonably fit for their purpose.

The problem outlined above shows that you have failed to fulfil these legal obligations and I have a claim against you for breach of contract. However, I am prepared to give you an opportunity to undertake the necessary remedial work to bring the spectacles to a reasonable standard within a reasonable time.

I expect you to do this within 14 days. If you fail to do so, I shall have no alternative but to retain another optician to put the matter right and look to you to bear the cost of the work, as I am legally entitled to do.

Yours sincerely

Requesting access to medical records

Dear

[Reference: record holder's name and practice]

I would like to see my medical records. I understand that I am entitled under the Access to Health Records Act 1990 to see paper medical records concerning me that were written on or after 1 November 1991, and that the Data Protection Act 1998 entitles me to see medical records relating to me that are held on computer.

My medical records will have been updated within the last 40 days as a result of treatment I received from you on **[date]** for **[describe]**. I am therefore entitled to access to my records free of charge, and I would like a copy of them sent to me direct.

Although I have no right of access to information recorded on paper before 1 November 1991, I would also like to see a copy of previously recorded paper records. I hope that you are willing to show me these records on an informal basis, and I look forward to hearing from you shortly.

Yours sincerely

Writing to an NHS Trust hospital's complaints manager about the length of time spent on the waiting list

Dear

I am writing to you to complain about the amount of time I have had to wait for treatment for my condition **[describe]**.

On **[date]** my GP **[name and address of practice]** wrote to **[name of the specialist]** referring me to the specialist for treatment. The specialist first saw me as an outpatient at your hospital on **[date]** and decided that it was necessary to admit me to hospital. I was therefore put on the appropriate waiting list. However, I am still waiting to be admitted to the hospital for treatment.

The NHS's published goals say that I should expect to wait no more than 18 months before I am admitted. It is now later than that. You have therefore failed to meet the standard set out in *Your Guide to the NHS*.

As you can appreciate, I am anxious to be treated and so expect you to fix an appointment for my admission to hospital straightaway. I therefore look forward to hearing from you within the next seven days.

Yours sincerely

Complaining to an NHS Trust hospital's complaints manager about poor outpatient treatment

Dear

I am writing to you to complain about the amount of time I have had to wait for treatment from your outpatients' clinic.

On **[date]** my GP **[name and address of practice]** wrote to **[name of specialist]** referring me to the specialist for treatment for my condition **[describe]**. On **[date]** the hospital wrote to me confirming an appointment on **[date and time]**. Although I arrived at the clinic in good time, I was ignored for a considerable amount of time. When I asked what was happening I was told that the specialist could not see me until **[time]**. When I complained about the long delay, I was given no explanation or apology.

Since the delay was considerable, I would like you to look into this matter and explain what happened.

I look forward to hearing from you in due course.

Yours sincerely

Writing to an NHS Trust hospital's complaints manager about a postponed operation

Dear

I am writing to you to complain about the postponement of my scheduled operation for my condition **[describe]**.

As you will know from your records, my operation was scheduled to take place on **[date]**. However, when I arrived at the hospital on that day I was told that my operation had been cancelled because **[describe circumstances]**. I was also told that you would contact me to fix another date for the operation.

As you can appreciate, the late cancellation of the operation has caused me considerable inconvenience and distress.

I am anxious that the operation should take place soon and so expect you to fix another appointment straightaway. I therefore look forward to hearing from you within the next seven days.

Yours sincerely

Chapter 14

Neighbours

Whatever kind of problem you are experiencing with your neighbours, first try to sort it out amicably with them. If a reasonable direct approach does not work, take formal action. You will need evidence substantiating your claim, so keep a detailed diary of each incident or disturbance.

As a householder, you have certain rights over your property; similarly your neighbours have such rights over their property. At times, these rights may clash. This is when you can call upon the law to step in so that the dispute may be resolved, particularly if you are faced with what is defined as a nuisance – see below.

If your neighbours are a nuisance and you have failed to settle your differences, you can in some circumstances complain to your local council, which may prosecute your neighbour under criminal law. Alternatively, you might take action yourself under civil law.

A word of warning, though: behaviour that annoys you need not be a nuisance in the legal sense, and so you need to be sure that you really have a case. Strictly speaking, 'nuisance' means unlawful interference with someone else's enjoyment of their own land. Bear in mind, too, that civil cases can be very expensive, so before embarking on court action you should consult a solicitor. Alternatively, why not try one of the many local mediation schemes, which aim to resolve disputes through discussion. Mediation UK★, for example, can put you in touch with a scheme in your area.

Noisy neighbours

If you are bothered by noisy neighbours, contact the Environmental Health Department of your local authority. You will have to satisfy them that the noise is unreasonably loud, is disturbing your sleep or is interfering with your enjoyment of your property, and so amounts to a legally defined nuisance. After investigation, the council may serve a notice on the neighbours forbidding the playing of loud music, say, or limiting it to certain times or to more reasonable levels. If your neighbours continue, they risk a fine of up to £2,000 – plus a further £50 for every day that the nuisance continues unabated.

Alternatively, instead of approaching the local authority, you can go direct to the magistrates' court (sheriff court in Scotland). Again, you will need evidence, and will have a better chance of success if you get statements from other neighbours, or even a doctor's note saying the noise is affecting your health. Your neighbours may be fined if the noise continues.

You can seek an injunction (an interdict in Scotland) in the county or High Court (sheriff court in Scotland) forbidding the neighbour to continue the disturbance. The advantage of this is that you can also claim compensation for the annoyance and disturbance you have suffered. But the procedure can be very expensive, so you should consult a solicitor before applying for an injunction.

Also, the Noise Act 1996 gives local authorities additional powers to deal with loud noise coming from domestic premises between 11pm and 7am. The Act created a new night-time criminal offence: offenders are liable to £100 on-the-spot fines; hi-fi equipment, say, can be confiscated; and there is a maximum £1,000 fine in cases that come to court. Councils in England and Wales can use the law at their discretion to tackle noise problems. Complaints should be made to your local Environmental Health Department. If poor insulation is to blame, the Environmental Health Officer can serve a notice on the property owner demanding improvements.

Bonfires

Whether bonfires constitute a legally defined nuisance depends on whether they interfere with anyone's use and enjoyment of their own property, and whether the bonfires are lit more frequently than an ordinary person would consider reasonable. Occasional bonfires may not constitute a nuisance. But if you consider someone's frequent bonfires unreasonable, keep a detailed diary of when they are lit and get statements from other people affected by them.

If you cannot persuade your neighbour to be more reasonable, contact your local Environmental Health Department. It can serve a notice on your neighbour requiring the lighting of the fires to stop (though this is unlikely), or to occur less frequently, or even requiring the site of the bonfires to be moved to a different area of the garden. If your neighbour ignores the notice, the local authority could take him to the magistrates' court. If found guilty, your neighbour would be liable to a fine, fixed by the court, of up to £2,000 plus a daily penalty, currently £50, if he continues causing a nuisance.

You can bypass the local authority and go straight to the magistrates' court yourself to ask for a 'nuisance order'. This is similar, in effect, to the action taken by the local authority. But remember that you will have to prove your case, so make sure that you have evidence supporting your case: a diary of events, other neighbours' statements and so on.

Overhanging branches

You are legally entitled to cut off any branches overhanging your property at the point where they cross the boundary. Technically you must offer them back to your neighbour, as the branches remain his or her property. (This applies equally to any fruit trees whose fruit-laden branches dangle temptingly over the garden fence.)

A word of warning: the tree may be subject to a Tree Preservation Order, so before you start lopping check with your local authority. If the tree is protected, you will need consent from the appropriate authority before you do any cutting. And if you live in a Conservation Area, you should ask the local authority before you start lopping the tree: the authority has six weeks in which to decide whether or not to issue a Tree Preservation Order.

If cutting the branches was intended to increase light to your property, but fails to do so, there may be very little else you can do. You do not have a right to light; you can acquire a right to light by express agreement with your neighbour (which is unusual) or by long usage – because you have received a certain level of light for at least 20 uninterrupted years, say. But this applies only to particular windows in your home, never to gardens. Even then, you have no redress if it is a natural object like a tree that is blocking the light.

Neighbours can also suffer problems caused by high garden hedges – especially leylandii. The Anti-Social Behaviour Act 2003 deals with the problem of 'high hedges'. If your neighbour's hedge is more than 2 metres high and it acts as a barrier to light or access to your property you can ask your local authority for help. The local authority will aim to resolve the dispute by mediation. But if that doesn't work it can issue a remedial notice requiring the hedge to be reduced to 2 metres.

Root problems

If the roots of a neighbour's trees cause any damage to your property, your neighbour is liable, and you can claim compensation, by suing in court if necessary (see Chapter 17). The neighbour cannot avoid liability just because the tree was there before you occupied the house.

If the tree's roots have caused subsidence to your property, you will probably be covered for this damage by your buildings insurance; it is far simpler to make a claim under the policy than to sue your neighbour.

Neighbours' short cuts

Each time they walk across your garden, your neighbours are trespassing, unless you have invited them on to your property. If a friendly word does not stop your neighbours doing this, you are perfectly entitled to bar their way, in person if need be. If faced with repeated acts of trespass, you may apply to the county court (sheriff court in Scotland) to get an injunction (interdict in Scotland). You will need advice from a solicitor before doing this.

Moreover, if the neighbours cause damage to your property while trespassing, you can claim compensation. The size of your claim will depend on the number of times your neighbours have trespassed on your garden; the distress and inconvenience it has caused you; and whether your garden has been damaged. Damage to your prize flower-bed, for example, would give you a claim for greater compensation than if you were simply complaining about someone trespassing on your concrete drive. Keep a log of events and take photographs of any damage.

Complaining to a neighbour about noise

Dear

On **[date]** I was disturbed by unacceptable levels of noise in the form of **[describe]** coming from your house.

When I asked you to reduce the level of noise, your behaviour was unacceptable **[describe]**. The **[nuisance]** continued **[describe circumstances]** causing **[effect on you]**. This has occurred on **[......]** occasions over the past **[period]**.

I am therefore writing to let you know that I am unable to tolerate any further disturbance. If I am disturbed by **[nuisance]** once more, I will have no alternative but to sue you for compensation in the county court. I will also apply for an injunction restraining you from making a similar amount of noise in the future.

Yours sincerely

Complaining to the Environmental Health Officer about a nuisance caused by a neighbour

Dear

I am writing to complain about a nuisance caused by my neighbour **[name]** of **[address]**.

My complaint is as follows **[describe nuisance in detail]**. On **[......]** occasions I have asked my neighbour to desist, but he refuses to do so.

This level of disturbance is unacceptable to me. I am considering taking a civil action against my neighbour but before I embark on that course I would appreciate your help with this matter.

I look forward to hearing from you in due course.

Yours sincerely

Complaining to a neighbour about bonfires

Dear

You have lit a bonfire in your garden on [......] occasions during the last **[period]** and the resultant smoke adversely affects my enjoyment of my property as follows **[describe effects]**.

I have repeatedly asked you to stop making these fires, but you ignore my requests. I have therefore consulted a solicitor, who advises me that the bonfires are lit more frequently than would generally be considered reasonable and that their interference with my enjoyment of my property constitutes a public nuisance.

If you do not stop lighting the fires I will report the matter to the Environmental Health Department.

Yours sincerely

Informing a neighbour of an intention to prune an overhanging tree

Dear

I am writing to let you know that the branches of your [......] tree which overhang my property cause the following problem [**describe**].

Would you please let me know if the tree is, to your knowledge, protected by a Tree Preservation Order. If it is not, I shall exercise my legal right to cut off all the branches overhanging my property.

I look forward to hearing from you within the next 14 days.

Yours sincerely

Complaining to a neighbour about damage caused by tree roots

Dear

During the last **[period of time]** I have noticed the following problem **[describe]**, which was caused by the roots of the trees **[describe]** in your garden. An independent surveyor's report has confirmed that these roots are to blame and I enclose a copy of that report.

You are legally responsible for the damage to my property.

Please let me know within the next 14 days whether you are prepared to repair the damage, which you are welcome to inspect in advance. If not, I will have the work done by my own contractor and will look to you to pay the cost of the repair in full, as I am legally entitled to do.

Yours sincerely

enc.

Complaining to a neighbour about acts of trespass

Dear

I initially complained to you about trespass on **[date]**, and since then I have told you on a great many occasions that I do not want **[persons involved]** to trespass on my property. Nevertheless you persist in **[describe]**.

If you continue to commit this **[act of trespass]** I shall, in accordance with my legal rights, apply to the county court for an injunction restraining **[persons involved]** from so doing. I shall also put in a claim for the considerable distress and inconvenience which you have caused me.

Yours sincerely

Chapter 15

Local authorities

The structure of local government is complex. If you have a problem that falls within the remit of your local authority, first identify which department in the authority is responsible. Look in your phone book (local authorities often have whole pages devoted to their services) or find out from your local library, Citizens Advice Bureau, council officer or councillor 'surgery' (usually published in your local paper).

Before writing to complain, phone the relevant department and ask for the name of the official who would be dealing with your query. Alternatively, address your letter to the director of whichever department you need, such as the Director of Highways. (Writing to the director will get your letter to the right person in the end but not necessarily as quickly as you would like.)

Many authorities have published service commitments; if your authority has, it should state the standard of service you are entitled to expect. If your problem is still unresolved, ask for a copy of the complaints procedure (particularly if you have received poor personal treatment). It can also pay to see a local councillor at this stage. Finally, if you are still not getting anywhere, contact your Local Government Ombudsman★ (the Ombudsmen deal with complaints about poor administration). If the Ombudsman finds that you have suffered an injustice because of poor administration, the report of the Ombudsman's investigation will contain a recommendation on the action the Ombudsman expects the local authority to take.

Planning matters

Planning permission is intended to make sure a proposed development fits in with the locality. Local planning authorities administer day-to-day planning. Contact the Planning Department of your local authority to find out what the relevant planning body is for a particular proposal. In Northern Ireland it will be the Department of the Environment*. (At central government level, planning is the responsibility of various Secretaries of State. For example, the Transport Secretary deals with motorways and trunk roads in England.)

Generally, applications for planning permission should be made through the Planning Department at your local authority. Contact the relevant department if you are unsure whether or not planning permission is required for any work you intend to carry out on your property.

Also contact the planning authority if you want to object to a planning proposal. Planning Departments are required to notify all affected properties when an application is made. However, planning officers' interpretations of this can vary between notifying only next-door neighbours to notifying whole streets. So the first you may hear about a proposal may be through the local press.

There are plenty of cases where residents have managed to fight off planning proposals or get plans changed, but it often takes years of hard work. Even if you are unsuccessful in the end, you may still win concessions, such as environmental improvements that will lessen the impact of the developments.

Injury caused by tripping up on the pavement

If you trip up on the pavement and injure yourself, you may have a claim against the local authority for negligence, but you will have to prove that the pavement was in a state of disrepair and had not been maintained with reasonable skill and care. There are no hard and fast rules about the condition a pavement has to be in to be the cause of a claim. However, your claim will be stronger if the pavement is in a bad state of repair – as a rule of thumb, if paving slabs protrude by more than 2.5 centimetres (1 inch) from the general level of the pavement.

You will be able to claim for any financial losses you incur (cost of repairs to your clothes and time off work, for example) and your personal injury, for which damages could be high (get legal advice from a solicitor).

Contact your local authority to find out the name and position of the appropriate official to whom to complain.

Asking your local authority to introduce road safety measures

Dear

[Reference: name of road]

I am writing to ask you to consider introducing road safety measures, such as a traffic-calming scheme and zebra crossing on the above road.

My reasons for writing to you are as follows: **[set out nature of problems]**. Because of these problems pedestrians who use the road are in danger of being hurt and injured. In particular **[describe specific dangers, such as those faced by young children and the elderly]**.

As you can appreciate from the above, this is a serious problem and I very much hope that your officers are able to consider the options for dealing with it.

A petition from other concerned pedestrians and users of the road is attached.

I look forward to hearing from you in due course.

Yours sincerely

encs.

NOTE
It will pay to get local councillors and the local press involved at an early stage in this sort of campaign.

Asking your local authority to introduce residents-only parking

Dear

[Reference: name of road]

I am writing to ask you to consider introducing residents-only parking on the above road.

My reasons for writing to you are as follows: **[set out nature of problems, highlighting any traffic problems]**. As a result of these problems it is very difficult for residents to park on the road.

A petition from other concerned pedestrians and users of the road is attached.

I look forward to hearing from you in due course.

Yours sincerely

enc.

Complaining about poor refuse collection

Dear

I am writing to complain about the poor refuse service I receive from you.

Although the refuse in my street is supposed to be collected on **[days and times]**, it is not. The collectors come only on **[days and times]**. The refuse collectors also leave litter scattered every time they visit the street. This level of service is unacceptable and causes hygiene problems.

I therefore want you to investigate this problem and let me know what action you intend to take to rectify matters.

I look forward to hearing from you in due course.

Yours sincerely

Objecting to a planning application

Dear

[Reference: planning application for name and address of property]

I wish to object to the planning application that has been made by **[name]** in respect of building works that are intended to be carried out at **[address]**.

My objections to the application are as follows: **[detail, highlighting any conflict between the application and other plans for your area; any increase in traffic or noise and so on]**.

I want you to take these objections into account when considering the application.

I look forward to hearing from you in due course.

Yours sincerely

NOTE
When objecting to a planning application show as many factual objections as you can. Also get as much support and publicity as possible. Lobby neighbours, local councillors, write to local papers and so on.

Complaining to a local authority about injury caused by an uneven pavement

Dear

On **[date]** I tripped over a paving stone which formed part of the pavement of **[street]** with the following results: **[describe]**.

You are responsible for maintaining the pavements in good order. The condition of the above pavement **[describe]** is clear evidence that you are in breach of your legal responsibilities.

In these circumstances, I am legally entitled to claim compensation from you. As a result of your failure to maintain the pavement properly, I experienced the following **[describe: loss of wages, damage to clothes etc.]**. I therefore claim compensation of **[£......]** for financial loss plus **[£......]** compensation for pain and suffering.

I look forward to receiving your cheque for the total amount within 14 days. If you fail to reimburse me I shall have no alternative but to issue a claim against you in the county court for recovery of the money without further reference to you.

Yours sincerely

Complaining to a local authority about its handling of your problem

Dear

[Reference: nature of problem]

I am writing to complain about your handling of my problem **[describe]**.

As you will recall from your files, I first contacted you on **[date]** to complain about **[describe]**. Since then I have been in lengthy correspondence with you concerning the problem. On **[date]** you wrote to me saying that my complaint could not be resolved to my satisfaction for the following reasons **[describe]**.

I do not regard your response as satisfactory because **[describe, including any breach of charter standards]**. I am therefore referring the matter to you for your reconsideration.

If within 14 days you have not made a reasonable offer to settle my claim, I shall have no alternative but to refer the matter to the Local Government Ombudsman for **[area]**.

Yours sincerely

Complaining to a Local Government Ombudsman about a local authority's handling of your problem

---

Dear

[Reference: name of local authority]

I am writing to you about my dispute with the above local authority in respect of **[describe]**.

As you will see from the enclosed file of papers, I have the following problem with my local authority **[describe]**.

On **[date]** I wrote to the director of **[department]** asking for my case to be reconsidered. On **[date]** the director contacted me saying that my complaint could not be resolved to my satisfaction for the following reasons **[describe]**.

I do not regard the local authority's response as satisfactory **[describe]**. I am therefore referring the matter to you for investigation.

I enclose copies of all the relevant papers, and I look forward to hearing from you in due course.

Yours sincerely

encs.

Chapter 16

Other problems

This section looks at cancelling sales agreements, injury on someone else's premises, unsolicited phone calls, faxes and goods, timeshares and unfair small print. It also examines your right to see your personal records and deals with discrimination and human rights.

Cancelling a sales agreement made at home

The Consumer Protection (Cancellation of Contracts Concluded away from Business Premises) Regulations 1987 gives you a seven-day cooling-off period, during which you have the right to cancel a contract which is made during an 'unsolicited visit' by a salesperson to your home. An 'unsolicited visit' means that you have not expressly requested the salesperson to call: that includes appointments made as a result of unrequested telephone calls or after delivery of a card proposing a visit. If you initiated the salesperson's visit, you are not protected by the Regulations. However, if you receive an unannounced visit and agree to the trader's coming back another time, the subsequent visit is also classed as 'unsolicited'.

The Regulations currently apply to most cash and credit contracts over £35, but do not cover agreements for the sale of food and drink, or other goods supplied by regular delivery.

The salesperson must give you a notice of your cancellation rights at the time the agreement or offer is made. If he does not, the contract is null and void. In addition, the trader commits an offence if he fails to give you written notice of your right to cancel and a cancellation form for that purpose. Trading Standards Departments are responsible for enforcing the offence and the maximum fine is £2,500. You are not penalised for cancelling at any time within the cooling-off period. If you have paid a deposit you can demand its return. To cancel the contract, either send the cancellation notice or write to the trader, saying that you are cancelling the contract in accordance with your legal rights. You must keep the goods safe until they are collected by the trader.

Injury occurring on someone else's premises

If you are injured while on someone else's premises, whether it is a shop, station, office or private residence, you may be able to claim compensation. The occupiers of premises have a legal duty towards you, as laid down by the Occupiers' Liability Act 1957, Act (N.I.) 1957 and Occupiers' Liability (Scotland) Act 1960, to take reasonable care to see that you will be reasonably safe.

You will need to prove that you sustained your injury as a result of negligence on the part of the occupier of the premises. If the case went to court, it would be left to the judge to decide whether or not the occupier had failed to take reasonable care to see that you were reasonably safe. If for example, while in a shop, you slip on some spilt yoghurt and break your arm, you will have a strong case for compensation, provided the yoghurt had been there long enough for the shop staff to discover it and clean it up, or to put a sign up warning of the danger. If, on the other hand, the yoghurt had just been dropped by a customer and the shop had not had time to cordon off the area or clear up the mess, then you would not be able to prove negligence.

You can claim compensation for the time you have had to take off work, lost wages and the pain and suffering caused by the fall, which could be substantial depending on the seriousness of the injury, and 'loss of amenity'. This means that if you are a painter and decorator, and cannot use ladders for six months, for example, you will be entitled to claim more compensation than someone who does not have to climb ladders for a living. Get legal advice from a solicitor on how much to claim.

Junk mail

If you do not want to receive advertising circulars and other forms of junk mail by post, you can write to the Mailing Preference Service (MPS)★ to request that your name and address be removed from mailing lists of companies sending such material. This is a free service set up and funded by the direct mail industry to enable consumers to have the opportunity to have their names and addresses taken off or added to lists used by its members.

If you want to stop unsolicited mail from member companies, write to the MPS for an application form.

Unsolicited phone calls and faxes

There is a similar service to the Mailing Preference Service for unsolicited phone calls, and a complete ban on unsolicited faxes to private individuals. The Privacy and Electronic Communications Regulations 2003 provide the following protection for consumers:

- a complete ban on the sending of unsolicited advertising or marketing faxes to individual consumers unless consent has been given beforehand. Individual consumers now have the ability to opt out of receiving unsolicited direct-marketing phone calls by registering free of charge with a centralised list of subscribers who do not want to receive these calls. This is operated by the Direct Marketing Association*, appointed by the Office of Communications (OFCOM)*, under the Regulations. The register is known as the Telephone Preference Service. Companies that operate by direct marketing by phone or fax must offer a contact address or freephone number so that consumers can contact them to ask to be removed from their database
- the Information Commissioner* enforces the Regulations and any company breaking the Regulations faces a substantial fine. In addition, if you can show that you have suffered damage as a result of a breach of the Regulations, you are entitled to compensation. However, most claims will amount to little more than the extra expense of a letter or phone call, plus possible stress as a result (although this is never easy to quantify in terms of compensation), and it is unlikely that many compensation claims will succeed. The Commissioner has also issued best practice guidelines for collecting customer data for future marketing. Individuals must now opt in to any kind of direct marketing. The penalty for misuse of personal data is £5,000, or an unlimited fine for persistent offenders.

The Distance Selling Regulations 2000 also require telephone sales and marketing businesses that cold call consumers at home to give details of who they are and why they are calling at the start of the call.

If you receive text messages on your mobile phone giving you a premium-rate number to call to claim a prize you can report these to the Independent Committee for the Supervision of Standards of Telephone Information Services (ICSTIS). ICSTIS regulates the premium-rate phone and fax industry and it can fine and bar companies from using these high-cost lines.

Your rights to see personal information held about you

With regard to personal data held by companies you have the following rights:

- under the Consumer Credit Act 1974 you are entitled to see information held by a credit reference agency (see pages 159–60)
- under the Access to Health Records 1990 you are entitled to see your paper medical records written on or after 1 November 1991 (see pages 219–20)
- under Section 7 of the Data Protection Act 1998 you are entitled to see a copy of any personal data held on a computer, provided you make a written request to the holder of the information. The holder may make a charge of £10, and must respond to your request within 40 days. If you do not receive a reply you should complain to the Information Commissioner★. If there is an error in the records you can seek compensation through the courts for damage and distress. If the court is satisfied that personal data held by a company is inaccurate it may order rectification or erasure of that data, or the inclusion of a supplementary statement clarifying the matter. Contact the Information Commissioner if you have problems of this sort.
- the Data Protection Act 1998 also gives individuals rights in relation to any personal data that is held about them in some paper records (such as a card index, microfiche storage systems or details stored in a filing cabinet by surname).

The Freedom of Information Act

The Freedom of Information Act 2000 gives individuals the right to information from public authorities, for example central or local government, the police, health authorities. You have the right to know if a public authority holds the information you are seeking, and if it is not exempt information, you are entitled to receive it. Even exempt information may be disclosed if it is in the public interest. You may have to pay a fee to cover some of the costs of collecting the information or for a copy of a published report. The Information Commissioner oversees the working of the Act.

The Act came fully into force on 1 January 2005.

Unsolicited goods

If you receive goods that you have not ordered and do not want, sent in the hope that you will buy them, do not worry. The Unsolicited Goods and Services Act 1971, or, in Northern Ireland, the Unsolicited Goods and Services (Northern Ireland) Order 1976, makes this kind of sales technique illegal. Your options under the Act are either:

- to do nothing and keep the goods in a safe place for six months, after which time they become yours to keep. But if the sender wants the goods back during this period, he is entitled to them. You may not refuse to send them back if the sender pays the postage, nor may you refuse to allow him to collect the goods
  or
- to write to the sender giving notice that you did not ask for the goods to be sent, that you do not want them and that they are available for collection by the sender. If the sender does not then collect the goods within 30 days they become your property.

You should ignore all demands on the part of the sender of the goods for payment or to send the goods back, unless the sender pays the postage. You should report the matter to your local Trading Standards Department (in the telephone directory under local authority). Demands for payment in such circumstances are a criminal offence for which the sender may be prosecuted and fined.

Timeshare

The Timeshare Act 1992, as updated by the Timeshare Regulations 1997, provides for a 14-day (minimum) cooling-off period in timeshare contracts signed in the UK. The Act makes it a criminal offence for an operator to enter into a timeshare agreement without first giving you, the customer, notice of your rights to cancel the contract at any time during the cooling-off period. A cancellation form for you to complete and return should be attached to the notice setting out your cancellation rights. If you cancel during the cooling-off period, you are entitled to recover any money you have paid in connection with the contract.

The Act also provides for a minimum cooling-off period of 14 days in the case of most timeshare credit agreements – in other words, where there is a provision for credit with which to pay for the timeshare. As for timeshare agreements, the Act requires provision of a statement, to which a cancellation form should be attached, of your rights to cancel during the cooling-off period. The statement should also set out arrangements for repayment of credit should the agreement be cancelled. In line with other laws covering credit, it is not, however, a criminal offence to fail to hand over a notice of your rights to cancel a timeshare credit agreement.

If you sign a timeshare agreement elsewhere in Europe you will be entitled to a cooling-off period of at least ten days from the day you sign the timeshare contract. It is illegal for a seller to ask for any money from you upfront, so you can refuse to give a deposit. Also, you must be given information about the property in your own language.

Unfair small print

The Unfair Terms in Consumer Contracts Regulations 1999 sets out the law on unfair contract terms. The Regulations cover contracts with businesses that were made after 1 July 1995. They add to and do not replace existing protection for consumers, particularly that provided by the Unfair Contract Terms Act 1977 (see page 15).

The Regulations and the 1977 Act say that a consumer is not bound by a standard term in a contract with a seller or supplier if the term is unfair. If a term is 'unfair' it is invalid and will not affect your claim for redress. Only a court can say definitely whether a term is fair or unfair, but the decision would depend on whether:

- the term unduly tips the contract against the consumer and in favour of the business
- that imbalance amounts to a breach of the requirement of 'good faith'.

The Regulations say that businesses must write standard terms in plain and intelligible language.

The Regulations also give the Director General of Fair Trading (at the Office of Fair Trading)★ powers to stop the use of unfair standard terms by businesses, if necessary by obtaining a court order (an injunction). Since October 1999, as well as the Office of Fair Trading, Which?★, OFGEM★, OFWAT★, OFCOM★, the ORR★, local Trading Standards Departments, the Information Commissioner★ and now the Financial Services Authority are able to take action under these Regulations. If you think that any of the standard terms in consumer contracts are unfair, write to the Unfair Contract Terms Unit at the Office of Fair Trading. The Unit will investigate your complaint and this may lead to a change in the contract that the business uses in the future.

Discrimination when buying and using goods and services

Refusing a service to you as a person with a disability, or deliberately not providing it on the same terms and of the same quality, is against the law. This is laid down by the Disability Discrimination Act 1995. Among other things, the Act covers discrimination when buying and using goods and services (but excluding transport services, such as buses and planes). Included is discrimination by many businesses and services such as:

- shops, mail-order or e-commerce sites
- hotels, restaurants, bars, clubs and leisure centres
- personal finance suppliers, such as banks
- services offered by local councils, such as parks.

So, if you have difficulty eating, for example, because of a disability, it would probably be unlawful for a restaurant to ask you to sit at a cramped, out-of-the-way table when other tables are not taken.

In a few cases, an organisation would not be breaking the law where it is impossible to give people with disabilities exactly the same service as other people. If, for example:

- the safety of people would be put at risk
- the service for other people would be seriously disrupted
- there is a different way into a building for people with mobility problems, such as a side entrance.

The Disability Discrimination Act also says that service providers must take reasonable steps to improve access for people with disabilities. This could mean:

- changing the way a service is provided (for example, a theatre might provide a sign language interpreter at some performances for people with impaired hearing);
  or
- making changes to make it easier to get into and out of a building (for example, widening doorways or building ramps).

The law came into force in 2004, although many organisations made changes to their premises to improve access before this.

For further help and advice contact the Disability Rights Commission★.

Cancelling a contract signed at home

Dear

[Reference: contract number]

On **[date]** one of your salesmen came into my house and asked me to buy **[item]**. I had not asked him to call; his visit was entirely unsolicited. Although I was concerned about signing any documentation, I decided that the only way I could get rid of him was by signing a contract for **[item]**. Under the terms of the contract I paid a deposit of **[£......]**. I have now decided that I do not want the **[item]**.

I understand that the Consumer Protection (Cancellation of Contracts Concluded away from Business Premises) Regulations 1987 provide for a seven-day cooling-off period, during which consumers have the right to cancel contracts made during an unsolicited visit. I am hereby giving notice that I wish to exercise my rights under the Regulations and cancel my contract with you.

I look forward to having my deposit returned within seven days.

Yours sincerely

Claiming compensation for an accident on someone's premises

Dear

On **[date]** I was on your premises **[shop, office, etc.: address]** when the following accident occurred; **[describe]**.

From the nature of this accident and its cause **[describe: slippery floor, etc.]**, it is clear that your premises were not reasonably safe, and that you had failed to take reasonable precautions to make them so, as you are obliged to do under the terms of the Occupiers' Liability Act 1957. I therefore hold you liable for the accident and the pain and distress I have suffered as a result **[describe if necessary]**.

I am legally entitled to receive compensation from you and I look forward to receiving your proposals for settlement of my claim within the next 14 days.

Yours sincerely

Asking the Mailing Preference Service to remove your name from mailing lists

Dear Sirs

I am inundated with advertisements and other items of unwanted mail, all correctly addressed to me personally at my home.

I understand that I can ask to have my name and address removed from the mailing lists of companies that are members of your service. I therefore request that you remove my details from the lists forthwith.

Yours faithfully

Requesting access to personal data

Dear

[Reference: record holder's name and company]

I am **[state relationship to record holder, employee, customer, patient or student]** and I would like to see a copy of any personal data held on computer about me.

I understand that I am entitled under Section 7 of the Data Protection Act 1998 to see records concerning me that are held on computer.

You are therefore required by the above Act to provide this information within the following 40 days.

I look forward to hearing from you shortly.

Yours sincerely

Asking the sender of unsolicited goods to arrange for their return

Dear Sir

[Reference: brief description of goods]

On **[date]** I received **[describe goods]** from your firm which I did not order and do not want.

These unsolicited goods are available for collection upon reasonable notice from the above address. Please let me know what arrangements you intend to make for their collection.

Yours faithfully

Cancelling a timeshare agreement

Dear Sir

[Reference: agreement number]

I hereby give notice that I wish to cancel my timeshare agreement.

Yours faithfully

Complaining to the Office of Fair Trading about unfair small print

Dear

[Reference: business name]

I wish to complain about the unfair terms contained in the consumer contract used by the above business.

As you will see from the enclosed copy correspondence, I am in dispute with the business in the following respects: **[describe]**. In response to my claim the business has said that it is not responsible to me because of its standard terms and conditions. In particular, the business has referred me to clause(s) **[number]** of its contract, a copy of which I also attach.

I consider that the terms referred to above are unfair and unreasonable both under the Unfair Contract Terms Act 1977 and the Unfair Terms in Consumer Contracts Regulations 1999.

I understand that you are unable to intervene in this case, but I would ask you to look into this matter with a view to exercising your powers under the Regulations to stop the general use of the unfair standard terms used by this business.

Yours sincerely

encs.

Complaining about discrimination

Dear

On [date] I [ate a meal at your restaurant/ attempted to buy goods from your shop/tried to open a bank account at your branch].

I am a disabled person and the nature of my disabilities are **[short description]**.

As I tried to obtain the service/buy goods from you I was treated less favourably than other people without a disability. The reason why I feel I have been treated less favourably is as follows **[describe discriminatory treatment or why service was inaccessible]**.

When I complained at the time I was told **[describe]**.

The Disability Discrimination Act 1995 makes it unlawful for organisations to discriminate against people with a disability in the goods, facilities and services they provide. You are therefore breaking the law.

As a result of what happened I was unable to **[eat my meal in relative comfort/buy the goods/open an account]**. My feelings were also greatly hurt by the incident. I therefore expect you to **[set out what you want e.g. an apology, compensation for hurt feelings, undertaking to make changes]**.

I hope that we can resolve this matter amicably. However, if I do not receive your satisfactory proposals for settlement of my complaint within the next 14 days, I will refer the matter to the Disability Rights Commission.

Yours sincerely

Chapter 17

Going to court

Sometimes a letter will not resolve your dispute because the other party shows no interest in responding or causes delays – deliberate or accidental. In these circumstances you will be forced to threaten to take the matter to court.

If you have not used the small claims track before, read this chapter carefully. If you have used the small claims track before, you may still need to read this chapter as in April 1999 the whole court system was altered. However, it is still possible for individuals to take their own cases to court. In fact, every effort has been made to simplify the procedure and cut out some of the legal jargon which can make it difficult for laypersons to understand. The following sections outline how the new rules work.

Considerations before issuing a claim

Before issuing a claim you should consider the following.

- **Do you know the address of the company, firm or person?** The claim must be sent by post to the defendant's address: in the case of an individual his home address, in the case of a business the address the business trades from, in the case of a company its registered address (this can be obtained by contacting Companies House★ or Companies Registry★ in Northern Ireland).
- **Is the company, firm or person you are planning to sue likely to be able to pay the sum you are claiming?** For example, if a person is unemployed or a company has gone out of business they are not going to be able to pay what you are claiming (the judgment). However, if a company has gone out of business and you paid for goods or services over £100 with a credit card you will be able to sue the credit-card company.

- **Has the party you intend to sue already been taken to court by other claimants and not paid up?** You can check this by writing to the Registry of County Court Judgments★ enclosing a cheque or postal order for £4.50 for each name you are interested in. A search will be made of the Register of County Court Judgments and you will be told of any unpaid court orders.
- **Can you afford the fees?** You will have to pay a fee to start your claim. The fee is based on the amount you are claiming. You will also have to pay a fee if you have to file an allocation questionnaire (see pages 271 and 288), details of which can be obtained from court staff. If the court orders the defendant to pay the money you claim and he does not pay up, you will have to pay further fees to enforce your claim. These will be added to the amount the defendant owes you.
- **Are you prepared to travel to a court outside your locality?** If the defendant is based in another locality you may have to travel some distance. The amount you can claim for travelling and loss of earnings is limited. You will also have to pay for your witnesses to attend.
- **Can you afford the time?** Some cases are not defended but if yours is, you will have to take time to prepare your case, for example getting together documents, photocopying, taking witness statements, filling out forms and making one or maybe two attendances at court.
- **Do you need a solicitor?** Since neither party can claim for solicitors' fees, most people do not have a solicitor attending. However, if you are fighting a large company it may have the resources to employ a solicitor or barrister to prepare the case and attend the hearing. If this happens, as long as you have prepared your case well you should not be disadvantaged.

If in any doubt about the basis of your claim seek legal advice. Some types of case, such as personal injury claims, claims against professionals and building disputes, have a pre-action protocol, i.e. a procedure that the court will have expected you to follow before you issue your claim.

If you are concerned about speaking in court and you will not have a solicitor present at the hearing, you can take someone else to speak on your behalf. This person will be a lay representative and can be a relative, friend or advice worker. However, you must get the court's permission for someone to speak on your behalf.

Note that if you use an advice worker you may have to pay him, and you will not be able to claim those costs back.

Before proceeding, note these important points.

- **Beware of pursuing a case on the principle alone** Many people decide to take court action because it is the 'principle of the matter'. Beware of this, as you will not win a case if it is simply a matter of unfairness. You must have a legal basis for your claim and good arguments in support.
- **Damages are not to punish** Many claimants think that the court will make awards of damages against defendants to punish them (sometimes called punitive damages). This is not the case. A judge will consider your actual loss and whether it can be quantified financially. If your actual financial loss is minimal then this will be reflected in the damages awarded to you.

Cases are dealt with in line with what is known as the 'overriding objective'. This means dealing with cases justly, which includes case managing defended cases by allocating them to a track to ensure that they progress to a trial or final hearing as quickly and efficiently as possible.

There are three case tracks which apply. The small claims track in the county court deals with claims of £5,000 or less (except personal injury and housing disrepair where the limit is £1,000). The fast track deals with cases over those limits up to £15,000, and the multi track is for complex cases and cases worth over £15,000.

Whenever the court deals with a case, whether in the small claims, fast or multi track, it must do so in line with the 'overriding objective'. The aims are to:

- ensure the parties are on an equal footing
- save expense
- deal with the case in ways proportionate to the amount of money involved, to the importance of each case, to the complexity of the issues and to the financial position of each party
- encourage the parties to co-operate with each other
- identify the issues at an early stage, deciding promptly which issues need full investigation at a full trial and disposing of any others that can be dealt with earlier, and deciding the order in which issues are to be resolved

- encourage and facilitate the use of Alternative Dispute Resolution (ADR) procedures if appropriate, and help the parties to settle the whole or part of the case
- deal with the case without the parties needing to attend court, and making use of technology (e.g. video conferencing)
- give directions (instructions to the parties) to ensure that the trial proceeds quickly and efficiently.

The small claims track

The small claims track allows cases involving claims up to £5,000 (or £1,000 or less if the claim is for personal injury or housing disrepair) to be allocated to an informal and low-cost court process. Small claims are no longer 'automatically' allocated to the small claims court, but if the claim is for less than £5,000 it is likely that it will be allocated to the small claims track.

Why use the small claims track?

Cost is the main advantage to the claimant. Even if you lose, the only costs which normally can be awarded against you are those of the defendant's expert witness fees (up to a limit) plus out-of-pocket expenses of the defendant and witnesses (i.e. lost earnings and reasonable travelling expenses up to a limit). If you win, in addition to ordering that the defendant pay you money to meet your claim, the court will also order the defendant to pay any court fees you have paid, and you can ask to be reimbursed for your own expenses. You do not need a solicitor – this immediately saves you money – because you as claimant can easily deal with the appropriate documentation yourself. Free leaflets explaining what to do are available from county courts.

A letter before action

If your complaint is not getting anywhere despite your having followed the guidelines in this book, send a final letter before action threatening to issue a claim in the county court. In this letter, you put a time-limit on action by the other party, allowing, for example, seven days in which to send you your refund or compensation.

If your problem is not resolved by this course of action, you may have to issue the claim. But issuing a claim does not necessarily mean that you have to go to court. You can always pull out if the other party pays you or offers a satisfactory compromise. Issuing a claim shows that you mean business and often leads to a sensible offer.

Issuing (starting) a claim

Starting a claim is easy. You need three copies of the appropriate form N1 (the claim form). This is available from your local county court (look under 'courts' in the telephone directory). Alternatively, if you have access to the Internet you can start a claim online through Money Claim Online (*www.moneyclaim.gov.uk*). You can type the details of your claim directly on to the form and then print it out.

You will need three copies of the claim form – one copy for you, one for the court, and one for the person from whom you are claiming. If there is more than one defendant you will need a copy claim form for each.

On the first page of the form you give brief details of your claim. On the second page you must give fuller 'particulars' (details) of your claim. These should set out the basic facts of your case so that the court and the defendant know what the claim is about. Keep the particulars short and to the point – you may write or type your particulars on a separate page (see examples on pages 284–7). You will also have to sign a 'statement of truth' saying that the facts that you have put on the claim form are true.

You can take or send two copies of the form along to your local county court with a cheque made payable to 'HMPG' for the amount of the court fee. The fees vary depending on what amount you are claiming. You can get a leaflet from the court which will give the current fees.

When the claim form has been issued, the court will send you form N205A (notice of issue). This will show the date by which the defendant must reply.

The defence

Within a couple of weeks of receiving your completed claim, the court sends it to the defendant, who then has 14 days in which to submit a defence. If you do not receive notification of what is happening in this period, check with the court. If a defence is not filed with the court within 14 days of the claim being served on the defendant, you can apply to have judgment given automatically ('in default'). You will need form N14 – Request for Entry of Judgment in Default Action – which is available from the court. Write to the court, enclosing the completed form N14 sent to you by the court when the claim was issued. Following receipt of these documents, the court will enter judgment in default and will write to you saying that judgment has been so entered. You can then take steps to get your money (see below).

Allocation questionnaire

If the claim is defended you will be sent a copy of the defendant's defence and form N150 (the allocation questionnaire). The information on the allocation questionnaire is to help the judge decide which of the three tracks is most appropriate for your case – although you and the defendant can express a preference on this matter, the ultimate decision rests with the judge.

Filling out the allocation questionnaire

You will be expected to co-operate with the defendant or the defendant's solicitor when you complete the allocation questionnaire. Therefore, if the defendant does not contact you, you should contact him to see if you can agree the following:

- which is the most appropriate track
- how long you think the trial will take
- when to exchange evidence
- whether you should use the same expert.

The allocation questionnaire must be returned to the court by the date printed on the form, which will usually be within 14 days or less of receiving it.

Alternative Dispute Resolution The allocation questionnaire also asks whether the parties have considered Alternative Dispute Resolution (ADR). If you have not considered ADR up until this stage, now is the time to suggest to the defendant that you try to resolve the dispute by this method. The court will stay (suspend) the action for one month so that the parties can try to reach an agreement without having to go to court.

Expert reports Expert evidence is only allowed at a small claims track hearing if the judge gives permission. Ask for this in the questionnaire. You should not normally get an expert's opinion, or report, until the judge has given permission, otherwise if the judge refuses permission you will have to pay the entire expert costs yourself.

However, it can sometimes be helpful to get an expert report before this stage – if the other party agrees to abide by the opinion of an agreed expert the case can be resolved without going to court. Also note that the amount you can claim for experts is limited (to £200 at present).

Allocation When you return the allocation questionnaire, the judge will decide which track to allocate the case to after taking into account how much is in dispute. The court will write back and let you know the date of the hearing and give a timetable for you to follow (see below).

The court may tell you that the case has been transferred to another court and/or give you a date for a preliminary hearing.

Where will my case be heard?

Although you can start your claim in any county court in England or Wales, the claim will be heard in the defendant's local county court if the claim is for a fixed amount and the defendant is an individual. Alternatively, if the claim is not for a fixed amount (unspecified), the defendant may ask to transfer the case to his local court. If the defendant makes an application to do so the court may ask you to put forward reasons why the case should be heard in your local court before making its decision.

After allocation to the small claims track

Once the court has decided to allocate your case to the small claims track it will send you form N157 or form N160, which will tell you what you have to do to prepare for the final hearing. These are called directions and usually include the following.

- The court will usually give a direction regarding sending copies of documents (including experts' reports) on which you intend to rely to the court (called filing) and to the defendant, usually 14 days before the hearing date. Note that video evidence (e.g. a wedding video) can be relied upon.

- If you are calling witnesses, the court may direct that you prepare signed witness statements for each of them; again, these should be filed with the court and sent to the defendant.

Exchanging documents

Each side has to prepare a set or list of documents relevant to the case. You should include everything other than privileged documents (these are generally letters between you and your legal adviser). These sets or lists then have to be exchanged with the defendant who in turn has to make a similar set available to you. A standard form to accompany these sets is available from county court offices. Exchanging documents in this way lets you and the defendant know the precise basis of each other's case.

The sort of documents you should disclose are copies of your letters of complaint and the defendant's replies, copies of receipts for expenses you wish to claim and copies of estimates for the cost of repairing faulty work, for example.

Looking at the defendant's documents

When you receive the defendant's list of documents, each document that is not privileged (and therefore has to be disclosed) should be listed and dated: (1) letter to the manufacturer, (2) letter to you, and so on. You should ask to see any documents that you have not already seen, such as letters sent from the defendant to other parties (letters from a shop to its supplier about faulty goods you have bought, for example).

The preliminary hearing

The judge may not fix a hearing date at the allocation stage, and may decide to hold a preliminary hearing or propose that the case is dealt with without a hearing. The judge may hold a preliminary hearing if:

- the claim requires special steps that need to be explained personally to you and the defendant

or

- the judge considers that either you or the defendant has no prospect of winning

or

- your particulars of claim do not show reasonable grounds for bringing or defending a claim.

Preparation for the hearing

- Make sure you have complied with all the directions.
- If you do not disclose all your documents to the defendant within the relevant timescale you may not be allowed to use them as evidence.
- Remember to take original documents along to court.
- It is a good idea to take a list of all the points you wish to make so that you do not forget anything important.
- Make sure your witnesses know where the court is. Arrange to meet them beforehand.
- Take a pen and paper to make a note of the judgment.

If the case is settled before the hearing

If the defendant has a solicitor, the solicitor may ask you to draw up a consent order. This will be an agreement, signed by both parties, which sets out the grounds on which the parties have agreed to settle the claim. The order can be filed at the court. You should ensure that the order says that the claim will be stayed (halted) until the defendant complies with the terms of the agreement completely. This means that the claim can be resurrected if the defendant fails to carry out the terms of the settlement.

The hearing

The hearing takes place in public, before a district judge, and so members of the public can sit in. District judges differ in their approaches – some ask questions, others simply listen without intervening. You will be asked to present your case. Keep it simple and stick to the particulars you gave when the claim was issued. You will also be asked to call any witnesses you may have (such as an electrical expert, for example, confirming that your new hi-fi is inherently defective). The defendant will then give his side of the story and you will be given the opportunity to ask questions. The defendant may also call witnesses. Once each side has presented his evidence the district judge will make an order called a judgment.

The district judge will usually give a judgment there and then. If you win your case, in addition to being awarded all or part of your claim (depending on the judge's decision), you will also be awarded costs including court fees, costs relating to any witnesses and travel expenses from the defendant.

After the hearing

The court will send both parties an order setting out the judge's decision.

What if I cannot attend the hearing?

If you are unable to attend, write to the court and ask the judge to make a decision in your absence based on your documentary evidence alone.

If you fail to attend and lose

If you miss the hearing and the judge makes an order against you, you can make an application to have the judgment set aside and the claim reheard. But you must act quickly and make the application no more than 14 days after receiving the judgment. The judge will only grant the application if you had a good reason for not attending and you have a reasonable prospect of being successful.

Appeals

You have only 14 days from the date you receive the order to appeal. You must send a notice of appeal showing that there was either a serious irregularity or that the court made a mistake of law, and set out the reasons in support. There can be no appeal on an issue of fact. However, you should take legal advice before deciding to appeal because there will often be a hearing before a higher judge. If you lose your appeal, you may have to pay the costs of the other party, including any solicitors' costs, which could be substantial. The judge can dismiss your application to appeal without a hearing, but must give brief reasons for doing so.

What if the defendant does not pay up?

You may have to take action to enforce your judgment by one of the following methods:

- a warrant of execution
- an attachment of earnings order
- a garnishee order
- a charging order.

You will have to pay a fee for the above methods of enforcement, and this fee will be added to the money the defendant already owes you.

If you do not know anything about the defendant's finances, you can find out more by asking for an oral examination. This can help you to find out if the defendant can pay and which of the above methods is most suitable.

Warrant of execution (only suitable for claims under £5,000)
This gives the court bailiffs the authority to take goods from the defendant's home or business. The bailiffs will first try to collect the money you are owed, but if they fail to do so they will take goods to sell at auction. This type of order can be used against a business. For more information read the court leaflet *How do I ask for a warrant of execution?*

Attachment of earnings order
This type of order is suitable only if the defendant is an employed individual. It is not suitable if the defendant is a business as the order is sent to the defendant's employer. It instructs the employer to take an amount from the defendant's earnings each payday and send it to a collection office. The money is then forwarded to you. For more information read the court leaflet *How do I ask for an attachment of earnings order?*

Garnishee order
A garnishee order can be sent to anyone who owes the defendant money. Usually it is sent to a defendant's bank or building society which will freeze the account, but if the account is overdrawn on the day the order is received you cannot be paid. This type of order can be used for a business. However, you will need to know where the company banks and details of its account number, and be certain that on the day the order is received there will be money in that account. For more information read the court leaflet *How do I ask for a garnishee order?*

Charging order

This order prevents the defendant from selling his assets, such as land, property or investments, without paying what you are owed. The difficulty is that you will not get your money until the asset is sold. For more information read the court leaflet *How do I ask for a charging order?*

Oral examination

Apart from the warrant of execution, the above methods of enforcement require knowledge of the defendant's financial situation. An oral examination is not a method of enforcement but a way of finding out about the defendant's assets. This should help you to decide which method of enforcement is most suitable.

Additional help for disabled court-users

If you have a disability which may make going to court difficult, contact either the Customer Service Officer of the court or the Court Service★ Disability Helpline. There is also a Minicom service if you are deaf or hard of hearing.

Court errors

Complaints about administrative errors in the courts are fairly common. Court staff may have made an error listing your case, they may have mislaid your papers, there may have been delays in issuing court papers, and so on.

People complaining about administrative errors in the courts have some means of redress. These include (depending on the nature of the complaint): lodging appeals within the court structure; judicial review; and writing to the Chief Clerk, or the Court Service★ (the executive agency which administers most of the court structure).

The Charter for Court Users also now covers consumers' rights. The Charter covers your role as a juror, a witness or defendant in a criminal case in the Crown Court, and has special standards for divorce and family cases. It also lists what you can expect if you have anything to do with the county court (including the small claims court) or the High Court. For example, if you have made a claim in the county court, you can expect:

• to have the case heard in court within 40 days once you have told the court you are ready for trial

- to be sent a copy of the court's decision within ten days
- a response to your letters to court within ten days
- to have any written complaint acknowledged within two working days and a reply within 20 days from the date the court receives your complaint.

Magistrates' courts have their own charters administered by local magistrates' courts committees.

Complaints about bad service (but not the outcome of your case) should be made first to the court's Customer Service Officer. You should make further complaints in writing to the Court Manager. If you are not happy with the reply, write to the Group Manager. The name and address of both will be displayed in your local court office. If you are still not happy, you can write to the Court Service Customer Service Unit asking for an independent investigation. You can ask the Court Manager for compensation if you have lost money as a result of a mistake made by the court staff. Large financial claims will be referred to the Customer Service Unit of the Court Service.

As far as bad decisions by judges are concerned, the way in which you get redress is by appealing against the decision which you think is wrong. Always get legal advice before considering an appeal since the costs involved may be substantial.

If you want to complain about the way a judge personally has treated you in court (apart from the decisions made in your case), you should write to the Department for Constitutional Affairs★. You should give the name of the court, the court case number, the date of the hearings, the name(s) of the judge(s) concerned and the reasons for your complaint.

A 'letter before action'

Dear

[Reference: if any]

Further to my letter of **[date]**, to which you have not replied, I now write to inform you that, unless I receive your satisfactory proposals for settlement of my outstanding claim within seven days of the date of this letter, I intend to issue a claim against you in the county court without further reference to you.

Yours sincerely

A 'letter before action' in a personal injury claim

Dear

[Reference: if any]

I am again writing to you in connection with my claim for damages in respect of the **[accident at work/road traffic accident/tripping accident]** which occurred on **[date]** at **[place of accident]**.

Please confirm the identity of your insurers, if you have any.

As I have mentioned before, the circumstances of the accident are **[brief outline]**.

This accident happened as a direct result of your fault. The reasons for this are **[describe reasons e.g. defective machine, broken paving slabs]**.

As a result of the accident I suffered the following injuries: **[describe injuries and any treatment received]**.

Unless I receive your satisfactory proposals for settlement of my outstanding claim within seven days of the date of this letter, I intend to issue a claim against you in the county court without further reference to you.

A copy of this letter is attached for you to send to your insurers as it may affect your insurance cover and/or the conduct of any subsequent legal action if you do not send this letter to them.

Yours sincerely   enc.

A 'letter before action' suggesting Alternative Dispute Resolution (ADR)

Dear

[Reference: if any]

I am again writing to you in connection with my claim for compensation in respect of the **[briefly describe claim]**.

Please confirm the identity of your insurers, if you have any.

As I have mentioned before, I am legally entitled to compensation from you.

Therefore, unless I receive your satisfactory proposals for settlement of my outstanding claim within seven days of the date of this letter, I intend to issue a claim against you in the county court without further reference to you.

In an effort to save further costs and unnecessary expenses, I am, however, prepared to refer this matter to a qualified mediator or other form of agreed Alternative Dispute Resolution (ADR) mechanism. Please let me know if this is acceptable to you and whether you have a preferred form of ADR.

Yours sincerely

Claim Form (N1)

Claim Form

In the

ANYTOWN

for court use only

| Claim No. | |
| Issue date | |

Claimant

Mrs Elizabeth Sprogett
2 Spring Gardens
Anytown
AO6 3BX

SEAL

Defendant

Mr Frederick Plummer
6 High Street
Anytown
AO1 2DY

Brief details of claim

The Claimant and Defendant entered into a contract for the Defendant to repair a leak in the Claimant's roof. The Defendant's work is faulty. The Claimant is claiming the cost of repairing the Defendant's faulty work.

SPECIMEN

Value

£4,000

Defendant's name and address			£
		Amount claimed	*£4,000*
		Court fee	*£100*
		Solicitor's cost	
		Total amount	*£4,100*

The court office at

is open between 10 am and 4 pm Monday to Friday. When corresponding with the court, please address forms or letters to the Court Manager and quote the claim number.

N1 Claim form (CPR Part 7) (01.02)   *Printed on behalf of The Court Service*

Claim No.	

Does, or will, your claim include any issues under the Human Rights Act 1998?   ☐ Yes   ☐ No

Particulars of Claim (attached)~~(to follow)~~

See particulars attached.

SPECIMEN

Statement of Truth
*(I believe)(~~The Claimant believes~~) that the facts stated in these particulars of claim are true.
* ~~I am duly authorised by the claimant to sign this statement~~

Full name   *ELIZABETH SPROGETT*

Name of claimant's solicitor's firm _____

signed _____   position or office held _____
*(Claimant)(~~Litigation friend~~)(~~Claimant's solicitor~~)   (if signing on behalf of firm or company)
delete as appropriate

Claimant's or claimant's solicitor's address to which documents or payments should be sent if different from overleaf including (if appropriate) details of DX, fax or e-mail.

© Crown copyright

Court Particulars – claiming the cost of repairing faulty work

Case No. _____

IN THE **[Name]** COUNTY COURT

BETWEEN:

[CLAIMANT'S NAME]   Claimant

AND

[DEFENDANT'S NAME]   Defendant

PARTICULARS OF CLAIM

1. At all material times the Defendant carried on business as a **[describe business]** at **[address]**.

2. By a contract in writing made between the Claimant and the Defendant, contained in or evidenced by the Defendant's estimate dated **[date and reference number]**, the Defendant agreed to **[describe nature of work]** for the sum of **[£......]**.

3. It was an implied term of the contract that the Defendant would carry out the work with all due care, skill and diligence and in a good and workmanlike manner and with materials which were of a reasonable quality.

4. In breach of the implied term set out in paragraph 3 above, the Defendant failed to carry out the work with all due care, skill and diligence and in a good and workmanlike manner and with materials which were of a reasonable quality.

Particulars of Breach

[Precise details of faulty work]

5. By reason of the matters set out above the Claimant has suffered loss and damage.

Particulars of Loss

Cost of remedial work **[£......]**

AND THE CLAIMANT CLAIMS:

Damages limited to **[£......]**

STATEMENT OF TRUTH

I believe that the facts stated in these particulars of claim are true.

Signed_____ Dated_____

To: The Defendant

    The District Judge

Court Particulars – claiming the cost of repairing faulty goods

Case No. _____

IN THE **[Name]** COUNTY COURT

BETWEEN:

[CLAIMANT'S NAME]   Claimant

AND

[DEFENDANT'S NAME]   Defendant

PARTICULARS OF CLAIM

1. At all material times the Defendant carried on business as a **[describe business]** at **[address]**.

2. By a contract in writing made between the Claimant and the Defendant, contained in or evidenced by the Defendant's estimate dated **[date and reference number]**, the Defendant agreed to supply the Claimant with a **[describe goods]** for the sum of **[£......]**.

3. It was an implied term of the contract that the goods should be of satisfactory quality.

4. In breach of the implied term set out in paragraph 3 above, the goods were not of satisfactory quality.

Particulars of Breach

[Precise details of faults in goods]

5. By reason of the matters set out above the Claimant has suffered loss and damage.

Particulars of Loss

Cost of repairs to goods **[£......]**

AND THE CLAIMANT CLAIMS:

Damages limited to **[£......]**

STATEMENT OF TRUTH

I believe that the facts stated in these particulars of claim are true.

Signed_____ Dated_____

To: The Defendant

     The District Judge

Court Particulars – claiming the cost of a disappointing holiday

Case No. _____

IN THE **[Name]** COUNTY COURT
BETWEEN:

[CLAIMANTS' NAMES]	Claimants
AND	
[DEFENDANT'S NAME]	Defendant

PARTICULARS OF CLAIM

1. At all material times the Defendant carried on business as a **[describe business]** at **[address]**.
2. By a contract made in writing between the Claimants and the Defendant **[date and booking reference]** the Defendant agreed to provide the Claimants with a two-week package holiday as detailed in the attached page of the Defendant's brochure for the price of **[£.....]**.
3. It was an express term of the contract that the Defendant would provide accommodation that was four-star standard in accordance with the Defendant's brochure description and all the facilities advertised would be available.
4. It was an implied term of the contract that the services would be provided with reasonable skill and care.
5. In breach of the express and implied terms set out in paragraphs 3 and 4 the Defendant failed to provide the package holiday that the claimants contracted for.

Particulars of Breach

i. The hotel was not four-star standard **[give precise details of problems with room and facilities, for example the room was small and basic and the toilet leaked]**.
ii. The service was not commensurate with four-star standard **[give precise details, for example the food was poor and portions inadequate and the claimants had to purchase meals outside the hotel]**.
iii. The gym advertised in the Defendant's brochure had not been built.

6. By reason of the matters set out above the Claimants have suffered loss and damage.

Particulars of Loss

a. Loss of bargain – the Claimants' holiday purchased for themselves was worth considerably less than the price paid.
b. Loss of enjoyment – the Claimants are entitled to damages representing the loss of enjoyment over the course of their holiday.
c. Out of pocket expenses.

AND THE CLAIMANT CLAIMS:

Damages limited to **[£......]**

STATEMENT OF TRUTH
I believe that the facts stated in these particulars of claim are true.

Signed_____ Dated_____

To: The Defendant
      The District Judge

Court Particulars – when suing both supplier and credit-card company

Case No. _____

IN THE **[Name]** COUNTY COURT
BETWEEN:

[CLAIMANT'S NAME]   Claimant

AND

[SUPPLIER'S NAME (1)]   Defendants

[CREDIT-CARD COMPANY NAME (2)]

PARTICULARS OF CLAIM

1. At all material times the First Defendant carried on business as a **[describe business]** at **[address]**. The Second Defendant is a bank and at all material times carried on the business of providing consumer credit through a credit-card scheme known as **[name of credit card]**. The Claimant is a consumer and at all material times was the authorised user of a credit card **[give account number]**, 'the card' issued by the Second Defendant under an agreement **[date]**.
2. By a contract in writing made between the Claimant and the Defendant, contained in or evidenced by the Defendant's order form **[date and reference number]**, the Defendant agreed to supply the Claimant with a **[describe goods]** for the sum of **[£......]**.
3. The Claimant paid the price of **[£.....]** for the goods with the card issued by the Second Defendant under pre-existing arrangements between the First and Second Defendants. The agreement between the Claimant and the Second Defendant was therefore a restricted-use debtor-creditor-supplier agreement falling within Section 75 of the Consumer Credit Act 1974. A copy of the Claimant's statement of account showing the payment made by the Claimant through the Second Defendant to the First Defendant is attached to these particulars of claim.
4. It was an implied term of the contract that the goods should be of satisfactory quality.
5. In breach of the implied term of our contract in paragraph 4 above, the goods were not of satisfactory quality.

Particulars of Breach

[Precise details of faults in goods]

6. By reason of the matters set out above the Claimant has suffered loss and damage.

Particulars of Loss

Cost of the goods **[£......]**

7. Pursuant to Section 75 (1) of the Consumer Credit Act 1974 the Second Defendant is jointly and severally liable with the Second Defendant for repayment of the price of the goods as set out in paragraph 6.

AND THE CLAIMANT CLAIMS AGAINST BOTH THE FIRST AND SECOND DEFENDANTS

Damages limited to **[£.....]**

STATEMENT OF TRUTH
I believe that the facts stated in these particulars of claim are true.

Signed _____ Dated _____

To: The District Judge
      The First Defendant
      The Second Defendant

Allocation questionnaire

To be completed by, or on behalf of,

ELIZABETH SPROGETT

who is [1st][2nd][3rd][   ][Claimant][Defendant]
[Part 20 claimant] in this claim

In the

ANYTOWN COUNTY COURT

Claim No.	
Last date for filing with court office	

Please read the notes on page five before completing the questionnaire.

You should note the date by which it must be returned and the name of the court it should be returned to since this may be different from the court where the proceedings were issued.

If you have settled this claim (or if you settle it on a future date) and do not need to have it heard or tried, you must let the court know immediately.

Have you sent a copy of this completed form to the other party(ies)?   ☑ Yes   ☐ No

A   Settlement

Do you wish there to be a one month stay to attempt to settle the claim, either by informal discussion or by alternative dispute resolution?   ☐ Yes   ☑ No

B   Location of trial

Is there any reason why your claim needs to be heard at a particular court?   ☑ Yes   ☐ No

If Yes, say which court and why?

Anytown

Work commitment of the Claimant's witness.

C   Pre-action protocols

If an approved pre-action protocol applies to this claim, complete **Part 1** only. If not, complete **Part 2** only. If you answer 'No' to the question in either Part 1 or 2, please explain the reasons why on a separate sheet and attach it to this questionnaire.

Part 1	The* _____ protocol applies to this claim.
*please say which protocol	Have you complied with it? ☐ Yes ☐ No

Part 2	No pre-action protocol applies to this claim.
	Have you exchanged information and/or documents (evidence) with the other party in order to assist in settling the claim? ☑ Yes ☐ No

D   Case management information

What amount of the claim is in dispute?   £ _____

Applications

Have you made any application(s) in this claim?   ☐ Yes   ☑ No

If Yes, what for?   _____   For hearing on   _____
(e.g. summary judgment,
add another party)

Witnesses

So far as you know at this stage, what witnesses of fact do you intend to call at the trial or final hearing including, if appropriate, yourself?

Witness name	Witness to which facts
Mr TOM SPROGETT (The Claimant's Husband)	The Claimant's husband can give evidence regarding the damage caused by the faulty workmanship.

Experts

Do you wish to use expert evidence at the trial or final hearing?   ☑ Yes   ☐ No

Have you already copied any experts' report(s) to the other party(ies)?   ☑ None yet obtained   ☐ Yes   ☐ No

Do you consider the case suitable for a single joint expert in any field?   ☑ Yes   ☐ No

Please list any single joint experts you propose to use and any other experts you wish to rely on. Identify single joint experts with the initials 'SJ' after their name(s).

Expert's name	Field of expertise (eg. orthopaedic surgeon, surveyor, engineer)
Mr JOHN WIDGET	ROOFING ENGINEER

Do you want your expert(s) to give evidence orally at the trial or final hearing?   ☐ Yes   ☑ No

If Yes, give the reasons why you think oral evidence is necessary:

continue over

Track

Which track do you consider is most suitable for your claim? Tick one box   ☑ small claims track   ☐ fast track   ☐ multi-track

If you have indicated a track which would not be the normal track for the claim, please give brief reasons for your choice

E   Trial or final hearing

How long do you estimate the trial or final hearing will take?   _____ days _____ hours _____ minutes

Are there any days when you, an expert or an essential witness will not be able to attend court for the trial or final hearing?   ☑ Yes   ☐ No

If Yes, please give details

Name	Dates not available
CLAIMANT	22 - 29 June 2003
TOM SPROGETT	22 - 29 June 2003

F   Proposed directions (Parties should agree directions wherever possible)

Have you attached a list of the directions you think appropriate for the management of the claim?   ☑ Yes   ☐ No

If Yes, have they been agreed with the other party(ies)?   ☑ Yes   ☐ No

G   Costs

*Do **not** complete this section if you have suggested your case is suitable for the small claims track **or** you have suggested one of the other tracks and you do not have a solicitor acting for you.*

What is your estimate of your costs incurred to date?   £ _____

What do you estimate your overall costs are likely to be?   £ _____

In substantial cases these questions should be answered in compliance with CPR Part 43

H Other information

Have you attached documents to this questionnaire? ☑ Yes ☐ No

Have you sent these documents to the other party(ies)? ☑ Yes ☐ No

If Yes, when did they receive them? *With letter before action*

Do you intend to make any applications in the immediate future? ☐ Yes ☑ No

If Yes, what for?

In the space below, set out any other information you consider will help the judge to manage the claim.

SPECIMEN

Signed *Esprogett.* Date *1 March 2002*

[Counsel][Solicitor][for the][1st][2nd][3rd][ ]
[Claimant][Defendant][Part 20 claimant]

Please enter your firm's name, reference number and full postal address including (if appropriate) details of DX, fax or e-mail

		if applicable
	fax no.	
	DX no.	
Tel. no. Postcode	e-mail	
Your reference no.		

4

Notes for completing an allocation questionnaire

- If the claim is not settled, a judge must allocate it to an appropriate case management track. To help the judge choose the most just and cost-effective track, you must now complete the attached questionnaire.
- If you fail to return the allocation questionnaire by the date given, the judge may make an order which leads to your claim or defence being struck out, or hold an allocation hearing. If there is an allocation hearing the judge may order any party who has not filed their questionnaire to pay, immediately, the costs of that hearing.
- Use a separate sheet if you need more space for your answers marking clearly which section the information refers to. You should write the claim number on it, and on any other documents you send with your allocation questionnaire. Please ensure they are firmly attached to it.
- The letters below refer to the sections of the questionnaire and tell you what information is needed.

A Settlement

If you think that you and the other party may be able to negotiate a settlement you should tick the 'Yes' box. The court may order a stay, whether or not all the other parties to the claim agree. You should still complete the rest of the questionnaire, even if you are requesting a stay. Where a stay is granted it will be for an initial period of one month. You may settle the claim either by informal discussion with the other party or by alternative dispute resolution (ADR). ADR covers a range of different processes which can help settle disputes. More information is available in the Legal Services Commission leaflet 'Alternatives to Court' free from the LSC leaflet line. Phone: 0845 3000 343

B Location of trial

High Court cases are usually heard at the Royal Courts of Justice or certain Civil Trial Centres. Fast or multi-track trials may be dealt with at a Civil Trial Centre or at the court where the claim is proceeding. Small claim cases are usually heard at the court in which they are proceeding.

C Pre-action protocols

Before any claim is started, the court expects you to have exchanged information and documents relevant to the claim, to assist in settling it. For some types of claim e.g. personal injury, there are approved protocols that should have been followed.

D Case management information

Applications

It is important for the court to know if you have already made any applications in the claim, what they are for and when they will be heard. The outcome of the applications may affect the case management directions the court gives.

Witnesses

Remember to include yourself as a witness of fact, if you will be giving evidence.

Experts

Oral or written expert evidence will only be allowed at the trial or final hearing with the court's permission. The judge will decide what permission it seems appropriate to give when the claim is allocated to track. Permission in small claims track cases will only be given exceptionally.

Track

The basic guide by which claims are normally allocated to a track is the amount in dispute, although other factors such as the complexity of the case will also be considered. A leaflet available from the court office explains the limits in greater detail.

Small Claims track	Disputes valued at not more than £5,000 except · those including a claim for personal injuries worth over £1,000 and · those for housing disrepair where either the cost of repairs or other work exceeds £1,000 or any other claim for damages exceeds £1,000
Fast track	Disputes valued at more than £5,000 but not more than £15,000
Multi-track	Disputes over £15,000

E Trial or final hearing

You should enter only those dates when you, your expert(s) or essential witness(es) will not be able to attend court because of holiday or other committments.

F Proposed directions

Attach the list of directions, if any, you believe will be appropriate to be given for the management of the claim. Agreed directions on fast and multi-track cases should be based on the forms of standard directions set out in the practice direction to CPR Part 28 and form PF52.

G Costs

Only complete this section if you are a solicitor and have suggested the claim is suitable for allocation to the fast or multi-track.

H Other Information

Answer the questions in this section. Decide if there is any other information you consider will help the judge to manage the claim. Give details in the space provided referring to any documents you have attached to support what you are saying.

5

Asking the Chief Clerk of the County Court to enter judgment in default

Dear

[Reference: case number]

I understand that the defendant's failure to file a defence within 14 days of the service of the claim entitles me to enter judgment automatically.

As 14 days have expired since the service of the claim and I have not received a defence, I enclose form N14 (Request for Entry of Judgment in Default Action), together with the case note and would be grateful if you would enter judgment in default accordingly.

Yours sincerely

encs.

Asking the Chief Clerk of the County Court to postpone the preliminary hearing

Dear

[Reference: case number]

I have just received your note of **[date]**, giving a date of **[date]** for the preliminary hearing in this case.

Unfortunately I will not be able to attend on that date because **[reason]**.

I would therefore be grateful if you would fix a new date. I should be able to attend court from **[date]** onwards.

I look forward to hearing from you in due course.

Yours sincerely

Asking the defendant to supply copies of documents for inspection

---

Dear

[Reference: case number]

Thank you for your letter of **[date]**, together with your list of documents.

I would like to inspect the following documents: **[give numbers]**. I understand that it is standard practice for the parties to exchange copies by post and I would ask you to send copies to me direct. I am prepared to meet the cost of postage and photocopying if necessary. I look forward to receiving copies of these documents within seven days.

Please let me know if there are any documents included in my list of documents which you wish to inspect. I will then send you copies. I understand that I am entitled to ask you for the cost of having such copies made.

Yours sincerely

NOTE
Documents are normally exchanged by post. If the defendant asks you to pay postal and photocopying costs you should agree. You, in your turn, are entitled to ask for any expenses you incur in providing the defendant with documents.

Informing the defendant that the case is discontinued following receipt of full and final payment

Dear

[Reference: case number]

Thank you for your letter of **[date]** proposing settlement **[describe]**.

I am pleased to accept your cheque for **[£......]** in full and final settlement of my claim against you.

I am therefore discontinuing my claim against you in the **[location]** County Court and am copying this letter to the court.

Yours sincerely

cc: The Chief Clerk **[location]** County Court

Requiring the defendant to pay the sum agreed by the court

Dear

[Reference: case number]

The adjudication in the above case is that I am to recover from you the sum of **[£......]** for **[damages etc.]** and **[£......]** for expenses, amounting to a total of **[£......]**.

Under the terms of the judgment the above sum is payable forthwith.

Unless I receive your cheque for **[total amount]** within seven days I shall issue enforcement proceedings against you. This may result in goods belonging to you being seized and sold to satisfy the judgment and costs.

Yours sincerely

Complaining to the Court Manager about court errors

Dear

[Reference: title of case and case number]

I wish to complain about the quality of service I have received from the court staff concerned with the administrative support in the above case.

I am enclosing copies of all the relevant correspondence in the case. As you will see from the file, the court staff have made the following administrative errors when dealing with the case: **[describe]**. The court also fell below the standards set out in the Charter for Court Users as follows: **[describe]**.

I now ask you to investigate this matter, and I look forward to hearing from you in due course.

Yours sincerely

encs.

Chapter 18

Scotland

Most of the rules which apply when you buy goods and services are broadly the same throughout the UK. For example, if you buy faulty goods or receive a substandard service, you have the same entitlement to redress north and south of the border. Rights covering buying goods in Scotland are covered by the Sale of Goods Act 1979 as they are elsewhere. If you receive a substandard service – faulty building work, damage by a dry-cleaner, photoprocessor, and so on – your rights in Scotland are covered by common law, rather than the Supply of Goods and Services Act 1982, which applies in England and Wales.

But there are some differences. If, for example, you have a claim for breach of contract you have six years from the date of the breach in England to start a claim but only five in Scotland. Also, once a buyer makes an offer to buy a property and this is accepted, the agreement is binding, unlike in England.

Small claims

In Scotland, the small claims limit for most consumer cases is £750. If you want to claim from £750 to £1,500, you should 'raise' a claim in the sheriff court using the 'summary cause' procedure. Claims for personal injury up to £1,500 are also dealt with as a summary cause. All claims for more than £1,500 must use an alternative procedure known as an 'ordinary action'. For more information, see the Scottish Court Service's leaflets *The Small Claim* and *The Summary Cause*.

Small claims cases are heard in the sheriff court. These are the main features of the procedure.

- It can be used for almost all consumer cases up to a value of £750.
- All you have to do to start your claim is fill in a simple form and pay a small fee (a sheriff clerk will tell you what the fee is).
- The person making the claim is the 'pursuer' rather than the claimant, and the person against whom the claim is made is called the 'defender' rather than the defendant.
- There is a strict limit on the bill you are likely to face if your claim is defended. If your claim is for £200 or less, there is a 'no expenses' rule – which means you only have to pay your own expenses, win or lose. If you claim more than £200, you will not normally have to pay more than £75 of the other side's expenses even if you lose.
- There will usually be a preliminary hearing when the case will often settle.
- If your case comes to a hearing, it should be informal. You will not need a solicitor and you will not have to worry about the usual technical rules about the presentation of cases.

If you want to begin an action in Scotland, obtain further information on the small claims procedure by reading *What is a Small Claim?*, available from your local sheriff court, before you proceed.

Chapter 19

Northern Ireland

Consumer rights and consumer law in Northern Ireland are virtually identical to those in England and Wales. For instance, shopping, holiday rights and so on, and consumer rights in respect of British Telecom are the same across the United Kingdom. However, there are differences. For example, complaints about gas are dealt with by the General Consumer Council for Northern Ireland★ rather than OFGEM★, which covers Britain (see Chapter 9 on Utilities). Electricity complaints are dealt with by the Office for the Regulation of Electricity and Gas (OFREG)★. Similarly, in Northern Ireland the equivalent of Trading Standards Departments is the Trading Standards Service of the Department of Enterprise, Trade and Investment★.

Any differences are noted in the preceding chapters dealing with your rights in specific circumstances.

Small claims

The small claims procedure in Northern Ireland is similar to that in the county courts in England and Wales (see Chapter 17). The main differences in the procedure are:

- the small claims court can be used for consumer claims up to £2000
- personal injury claims and road accident cases are not covered.

If you want to bring a small claim in Northern Ireland, obtain further information by reading *Small Claims – Northern Ireland*, a free booklet available from your local Small Claims Court Office (in the phone book under 'Court Service', 'Government' or 'Council for Voluntary Action'). For information on enforcement procedure and fees contact any Small Claims Court Office or the Enforcement of Judgments Office★.

Glossary

Alternative Dispute Resolution (ADR) A method or methods of resolving disputes by conciliation as an alternative to going to court.

Breach of contract A refusal or failure by a party to a contract to fulfil an obligation imposed on him under that contract.

Caveat emptor 'Let the buyer beware.' This legal principle applies to the sale of property, and means that the onus is on the buyer to ascertain the quality and condition of a property before proceeding with its purchase. In this instance, purchasers do not have the right to seek redress subsequently.

Civil law Law which is concerned with rights and duties that pertain to individual citizens. If you suffer loss because someone else transgresses these laws then you have a right to redress and are entitled to take that person to court.

Claim form A formal document issued by a court informing a defendant that a court case has been started and instructing him to do something, such as defend the case or pay a sum of money to the claimant.

Claimant The person bringing a civil case in court (*cf.* defendant).

Common law This kind of law is based on the decisions of the courts in actual cases and amounts to the use of precedent.

Contract Any agreement that can be enforced by law. It gives the parties who have made the contract certain rights and obligations. Contracts can be made in writing, by word of mouth or even without a single word being spoken or written. Every day people make contracts without putting them in writing – buying food in supermarkets or travelling by bus, for example. These have the same standing as written contracts and, like all contracts, are governed by the law of contract.

Cooling-off period   The interval in which you are legally entitled to cancel a deal or contract without being financially penalised.

Criminal law   Law which is concerned with offences against the public, such as the Trade Descriptions Act 1968. Criminal law affecting consumers is enforced by public authorities such as Trading Standards Departments. You cannot get compensation directly by reporting a criminal offence such as a false trade description, but it will give you added leverage with your complaint.

Defendant   The person against whom a civil court case is brought (*cf.* claimant).

Estimate   A rough, provisional guide to the price that a tradesman will charge once the work is complete.

Fitness for purpose   If you inform a retailer that you want goods for a specific purpose, then as well as being fit for their more general purpose, the goods should also be reasonably fit for the specific purpose. If they are not, you have a claim against the retailer.

Guarantee   A manufacturer's promise to resolve manufacturing problems in its products free of charge. Some offer your money back, others offer a free repair or replacement. Always check the wording of a guarantee to see what is included. Guarantees are in addition to your rights under the Sale of Goods Act 1979 and are not in any way an alternative to these rights.

Injunction   A formal court order requiring a person or organisation to do, or not to do, a particular act. If an injunction is not obeyed, the party concerned may be fined or sent to prison. It lasts as long as the court so decrees.

Judgment   The formal decision of a court.

Law of bailment   A common law (*cf.*) rule which applies when you leave goods with another person or body to be kept safely, taken care of by them and returned to you on demand. If goods are lost or damaged while the other person or body has them, they are liable to compensate you – unless they can prove that the loss or damage was caused through no fault on their part.

Letter before action   A final letter giving the defendant, whether an individual or an organisation, one last opportunity to settle a claim before a claim is issued.

Negligence   The breach of a legal duty to take reasonable care, resulting in damage to the claimant.

Nuisance   The unlawful interference with someone else's enjoyment of his home.

Paying under protest   If a purchaser makes it clear, preferably in writing, when paying for goods or services that he or she is 'paying under protest', the purchaser retains the right to bring a claim later if something is wrong, or later goes wrong, with the item or service.

Quotation   A firm indication, given before any work is started, of the price that a tradesman will charge once his work is complete.

Reasonable   Description used in legislation to give some definition to the period of time within which certain parties have rights to redress. In consumer matters it is used in legislation to describe the time during which goods can be rejected and a full refund demanded. As 'a reasonable time' is not a precise interval, but depends on the circumstances of each case, it is advisable for consumers to act to seek redress as soon as they can.

Rejecting goods   Indicating to a retailer that the purchaser does not want the goods in question and in accordance with legally defined rights is seeking a refund.

Reserving rights   Preserving the consumer's right, in letters or in verbal complaint, to bring a subsequent claim, if the problem is not resolved at this stage.

Satisfactory quality   A legal requirement that goods should work properly, be free from minor defects, safe, durable and, if new, look new and be in good condition.

Statute law   Legislation which consists of Acts of Parliament (for example, the Sale of Goods Act 1979) and Regulations and Orders made under the general authority of Acts of Parliament.

Time is of the essence   An expression used in contracts to make time a crucial element of that contract and entitle the consumer to cancel it and insist on a full refund of the price paid if goods are not delivered in accordance with these instructions, or if a service is not performed on time.

Without prejudice   A term added to documents, usually letters, which attempts to protect the writer from having the letter construed as an admission of liability or willingness to settle. Generally, nothing said in 'without prejudice' correspondence will be allowed in evidence should the matter come to court. It should not be used on any documentation which may be needed to prove a case, should the lack of appropriate response to a complaint mean that the issue is taken to court.

Addresses

Accident Line
Abbey Legal Protection Limited
1st Floor
17 Lansdowne Road
Croydon
Surrey CR0 2BX
Tel: (0800) 192939
Fax: 020-8730 2801
Website:
www.accidentlinedirect.co.uk

Action for Victims of Medical Accidents (AVMA)
Tel: (0845) 123 2352
Fax: 020-8667 9065
Website: www.avma.org.uk

Advertising Standards Authority (ASA)
Mid City Place
High Holborn
London WC1V 6QT
Tel: 020-7492 2222
Fax: 020-7242 3696
Website: www.asa.org.uk

Air Transport Users Council
Room K705
CAA House
45–59 Kingsway
London WC2B 6TE
Tel: 020-7240 6061
Fax: 020-7240 7071
Website: www.auc.org.uk

Air Travel Organisers' Licensing (ATOL)
Consumer Protection Group
Room K3
CAA House
45–59 Kingsway
London WC2B 6TE
Tel: 020-7453 6424
Fax: 020-7453 6431
Website: www.atol.org.uk

Alternative Dispute Resolution Group
Grove House
Grove Road
Redland BS6 6UN
Tel: 0117-946 7180
Fax: 0117-946 7181
Website: www.adrgroup.co.uk

Architects Registration Board (ARB)
8 Weymouth Street
London W1W 5BU
Tel: 020-7580 5861
Fax: 020-7436 5269
Website: www.arb.org.uk

Association of Bonded Travel Organisers Trust (ABTOT)
86 Jermyn Street
London SW1Y 6JD
Tel: 020-7930 2388
Fax: 020-7930 7718
Website: www.abtot.com

Association of British Insurers (ABI)
51 Gresham Street
London EC2V 7HQ
Tel: 020-7600 3333
Fax: 020-7696 8999
Website: www.abi.org.uk

Association of British Travel Agents (ABTA)
Tel: 020-7637 2444
Information line: (0901) 201 5050
(50p per minute)
Fax: 020-7637 0713
Website: www.abta.com

Association of Chartered Certified Accountants
29 Lincoln's Inn Fields
London WC2A 3EE
Tel: 020-7242 6855
Fax: 020-7831 8054
Website: www.accaglobal.com

Association of Independent Tour Operators (AITO)
133a St Margaret's Road
Twickenham
Middlesex TW1 1RG
Tel: 020-8744 9280
Fax: 020-8744 3187
Website: www.aito.co.uk

Association for Payment Clearing Services
Mercury House
Triton Court
14 Finsbury Square
London EC2A 1LQ
Tel: 020-7711 6200
Fax: 020-7256 5527
Website: www.apacs.org.uk

Association of Personal Injury Lawyers (APIL)
11 Castle Quay
Nottingham NG7 1FW
Tel: 0115-958 0585
Fax: 0115-958 0885
Website: www.apil.com

Association of Plumbing and Heating Contractors (APHC)
14 Ensign House
Ensign Business Centre
Westwood Way
Coventry CV4 8JA
Tel: 024-7647 0626
Fax: 024-7647 0942
Website: www.aphc.co.uk

Bar Complaints Commissioner
289–293 High Holborn
London WC1V 7HZ
Tel: 020-7242 0082
Fax: 020-7831 9217
Website: www.barcouncil.org.uk

British Acupuncture Council
63 Jeddo Road
London W12 9HQ
Tel: 020-8735 0400
Fax: 020-8735 0404
Website: www.acupuncture.org.uk

British Association of Removers (BAR)
3 Churchill Court
58 Station Road
North Harrow
Middlesex HA2 7SA
Tel: 020-8861 3331
Fax: 020-8861 3332
Website: www.removers.org.uk

British Carpet Technical Centre/ Wiratec (BCTC)
Wira House
West Park Ring Road
Leeds LS16 6QL
Tel: 0113-259 1999
Fax: 0113-278 0306
Website: www.bttg.co.uk

British Chiropractic Association
Blagrave House
17 Blagrave Street
Reading RG1 1QB
Tel: 0118-950 5950
Fax: 0118-958 8946
Website: www.chiropractic-uk.co.uk

British Complementary Medicine Association
PO Box 5122
Bournemouth
Dorset BH8 0WG
Tel/Fax: (0845) 345 5977
Website: www.bcma.co.uk

British Gas
Transco
Emergency tel: (0800) 111 999
Tel: (0845) 600 5100
Home Energy Care: (0845) 955 5404
Website: www.house.co.uk
www.centrica.co.uk

British Insurance Brokers Association
BIBA House
14 Bevis Marks
London EC3A 7NT
Consumer helpline: (0870) 950 1790
Website: www.biba.org.uk

British Retail Consortium (BRC)
2nd Floor
21 Dartmouth Street
Westminster
London SW1H 9BP
Tel: 020-7854 8900
Fax: 020-7854 8901
Website: www.brc.org.uk

British Standards Institution
389 Chiswick High Road
London W4 4AL
Tel: 020-8996 9000
Fax: 020-8996 7001
Website: www.bsi-global.com

British Wood Preserving and Damp-proofing Association (BWPDA)
1 Gleneagles House
Vernon Gate
Derby DE1 1UP
Tel: (01332) 225100
Fax: (01332) 225101
Website: www.bwpda.co.uk

BT
Sales, service and billing:
(0800) 800 150
Fault reporting: (0800) 800 151
Website: www.bt.com

Building Societies Association
3 Savile Row
London W1S 3PB
Tel: 020-7437 0655
Fax: 020-7734 6416
Website: www.bsa.org.uk

Building Societies Commission
Contact through the Financial Services Authority

Centre for Dispute Resolution (CEDR)
70 Fleet Street
London EC4Y 1EU
Tel: 020-7536 6000
Fax: 020-7536 6001
Website: www.cedr.co.uk

Certified Bailiffs Association
Ridgefield House
14 John Dalton Street
Manchester M2 6JR
Tel: 0161-839 7225
Fax: 0161-834 2433
Website: www.bailiffs.org.uk

Chartered Institute of Arbitrators
International Arbitration Centre
12 Bloomsbury Square
London WC1A 2LP
Tel: 020-7421 7444
Fax: 020-7404 4023
Website: www.arbitrators.org

Civil Aviation Authority (CAA)
CAA House
45–59 Kingsway
London WC2B 6TE
Tel: 020-7379 7311
Website: www.caa.co.uk

Commission for Racial Equality
St Dunstan's House
201–211 Borough High Street
London SE1 1GZ
Tel: 020-7939 0000
Fax: 020-7939 0001
Website: www.cre.gov.uk

Companies House
England and Wales
Crown Way
Cardiff CF14 3UZ
Tel: (0870) 333 3636
Website:
www.companieshouse.gov.uk

Companies House
Scotland
Argyle House
37 Castle Terrace
Edinburgh EH1 2EB
Tel: 0131-535 5800
Website:
www.companieshouse.gov.uk

Companies Registry
Northern Ireland
Registry of Companies
Credit Unions and Industrial and
Provident Societies
Waterfront Plaza
8 Laganbank Road
Belfast BT1 3BS
Tel: (0845) 604 8888
Website:
www.companiesregistry-ni.gov.uk

Construction Employers Federation
143 Malone Road
Belfast BT9 6SU
Tel: 028-9087 7143
Fax: 028-9087 7155
Website: www.cefni.co.uk

Consumer Complaints Service
Helpline: (0845) 608 6565

Council for Licensed Conveyancers (CLC)
16 Glebe Road
Chelmsford
Essex CM1 1QG
Tel: (01245) 349599
Fax: (01245) 341300
Website: www.theclc.gov.uk

Council of Mortgage Lenders (CML)
3 Savile Row
London W1S 3PB
Tel: 020-7437 0075
Website: www.cml.org.uk

Council for Registered Gas Installers (CORGI)
1 Elmwood
Chineham Business Park
Crockford Lane
Basingstoke
Hampshire RG24 8WG
Tel: (0870) 401 2300
Fax: (0870) 401 2600
Website: www.corgi-gas-safety.com

The Court Service
Clive House
Petty France
London SW1H 9HD
Tel: 020-7189 2000
Website: www.courtservice.gov.uk

Data Protection Commissioner
See Information Commissioner

Department for Constitutional Affairs (DCA)
Selborne House
54 Victoria Street
London SW1E 6QW
Tel: 020-7210 8614
Website: www.dca.gov.uk

Department of Enterprise, Trade and Investment for Northern Ireland
Netherleigh
Massey Avenue
Belfast BT4 2JP
Tel: 028-9052 9900
Website: www.tssni.gov.uk

Department of the Environment for Northern Ireland
Clarence Court
10–18 Adelaide Street
Belfast BT2 8GB
Tel: 028-9054 0540
Website: www.doeni.gov.uk

Department of Trade and Industry (DTI)
Enquiry Unit
1 Victoria Street
London SW1H 0ET
Tel: 020-7215 5000
Website: www.dti.gov.uk

Direct Marketing Association UK Ltd (DMA)
DMA House
70 Margaret Street
London W1W 8SS
Tel: 020-7291 3300
Fax: 020-7323 4426
Website: www.dma.org.uk

The Disability Rights Commission Helpline
Freepost MID 02164
Stratford upon Avon CV37 9BR
Tel: (08457) 622633
Fax: (08457) 778878
Website: www.drc-gb.org

Drinking Water Inspectorate (DWI)
Floor 2/A2
Ashdown House
123 Victoria Street
London SW1E 6DE
Tel: 020-7082 8024
Website: www.dwi.gov.uk

DVLA
Swansea
SA6 7JL
Tel: (0870) 240 0009
Fax: (0870) 850 1285
Website: www.dvla.gov.uk

energywatch
4th Floor
Artillery House
Artillery Row
London SW1P 1RT
Tel: (0845) 906 0708
Fax: 020-7799 8341
Website: www.energywatch.org.uk

Enforcement of Judgments Office
Bedford House
9–15 Bedford Street
Belfast BT2 7DS
Tel: 028-9024 5081
Fax: 028-9031 3520

English Community Care Association
145 Cannon Street
London EC4N 5BQ
Tel: 020-7220 9595
Fax: 020-7220 9596
Website: www.ecca.org.uk

Equal Opportunities Commission
Arndale House
Arndale Centre
Manchester M4 3EQ
Tel: (0845) 601 5901
Fax: 0161-838 1733
Website: www.eoc.org.uk

Federation of Communication Services Ltd *(mobile phone industry)*
Burnhill Business Centre
Provident House
Burrell Row
Beckenham
Kent BR3 1AT
Tel: 020-8249 6363
Fax: (0870) 120 5927
Website: www.fcs.org.uk

Federation of Master Builders
Gordon Fisher House
14–15 Great James Street
London WC1N 3DP
Tel: 020-7242 7583
Fax: 020-7404 0296
Website: www.fmb.org.uk

Federation of Tour Operators
1st Floor, Graphic House
14–16 Sussex Road
Haywards Heath
West Sussex RH16 4EA
Tel: (01444) 457 900
Fax: (01444) 457 901
Website: www.fto.co.uk

Finance & Leasing Association (FLA)
2nd Floor, Imperial House
15–19 Kingsway
London WC2B 6UN
Tel: 020-7836 6511
Fax: 020-7420 9600
Website: www.fla.org.uk

Financial Ombudsman Service
South Quay Plaza
183 Marsh Wall
London E14 9SR
Tel: (0845) 080 1800
Fax: 020-7964 1001
Website:
www.financial-ombudsman.org.uk

Financial Services Authority (FSA)
25 The North Colonnade
London E14 5HS
Consumer helpline: (0845) 606 1234
Tel: 020-7066 1000
Fax: 020-7066 1099
Website: www.fsa.gov.uk

Financial Services Compensation Scheme (FSCS)
7th Floor
Lloyds Chambers
1 Portsoken Street
London E1 8BN
Tel: 020-7892 7300
Fax: 020-7892 7301
Website: www.fscs.org.uk

General Chiropractic Council
44 Wicklow Street
London WC1X 9HL
Tel: 020-7713 5155
Fax: 020-7713 5844
Website: www.gcc-uk.org

General Consumer Council for Northern Ireland
Elizabeth House
116 Holywood Road
Belfast BT4 1NY
Tel: 028-9067 2488
Fax: 028-9065 7701
Website: www.gccni.org.uk

General Council of the Bar
289–293 High Holborn
London WC1V 7HZ
Tel: 020-7242 0082
Fax: 020-7831 9217
Website: www.barcouncil.org.uk

General Dental Council (GDC)
37 Wimpole Street
London W1G 8DQ
Tel: 020-7887 3800
Fax: 020-7224 3294
Website: www.gdc-uk.org

General Medical Council (GMC)
Regent's Place
350 Euston Road
London NW1 3JN
Tel: (0845) 357 8001
Website: www.gmc-uk.org

General Optical Council (GOC)
41 Harley Street
London W1G 8DJ
Tel: 020-7580 3898
Fax: 020-7436 3525
Website: www.optical.org

General Osteopathic Council
Osteopathy House
176 Tower Bridge Road
London SE1 3LU
Tel: 020-7357 6655
Fax: 020-7357 0011
Website: www.osteopathy.org.uk

Glass and Glazing Federation
44–48 Borough High Street
London SE1 1XB
Tel: (0870) 042 4255
Fax: (0870) 042 4266
Website: www.ggf.org.uk

Guarantee Protection Insurance
27 London Road
High Wycombe
Buckinghamshire HP11 1BW
Tel: (01494) 447049
Fax: (01494) 465194
Website: www.gptprotection.co.uk

Hairdressing Council
12 David House
45 High Street
South Norwood
London SE25 6HJ
Tel: 020-8771 6205
Website: www.haircouncil.org.uk

Healthcare Commission
Finsbury Tower
103–105 Burnhill Row
London EC1Y 8TG
Tel: 020-7448 9200
Website: www.chai.org.uk

Health Information Service
Tel: (0845) 4647 NHS Direct
(information on waiting times in your area)

Health Service Ombudsman
England
Eleventh Floor
Millbank Tower
Millbank
London SW1P 4QP
Tel: 020-7217 4051
Fax: 020-7217 4000
Website: www.ombudsman.org.uk

Northern Ireland
Parliamentary Ombudsman
Freepost BEL 1478
Tel: (0800) 343424
Fax: 028-9023 4912
Website: www.ni-ombudsman.org.uk

Scottish Public Services Ombudsman
4 Melville Street
Edinburgh EH3 7NS
Tel: (0870) 011 5378
Fax: (0870) 011 5379
Website:
www.scottishombudsman.org.uk

Wales
Fifth Floor
Capital Tower
Greyfriars Road
Cardiff CF10 3AG
Tel: 029-2039 4621
Website: www.ombudsman.org.uk

**Hire Purchase Information plc
(HPI)**
PO Box 61
Dolphin House
New Street
Salisbury
Wiltshire SP1 2TB
Tel: (01722) 422422
Website: www.hpicheck.com

HM Land Registry
32 Lincoln's Inn Fields
London WC2A 3PH
Tel: 020-7917 8888
Website: www.landreg.gov.uk

HM Treasury
Correspondence & Enquiry Unit
2/W1
1 Horse Guards Road
London SW1A 2HQ
Tel: 020-7270 4558
Website: www.hm-treasury.gov.uk

**Incorporated Society of Valuers and
Auctioneers**
See RICS

Independent Warranty Association
Spring House
51 Spring Gardens
Northampton NN1 1LX
Tel: (01604) 604511
Fax: (01604) 604512
Website: www.iwa.biz

Information Commissioner's Office
Wycliffe House
Water Lane
Wilmslow
Cheshire SK9 5AF
Tel: (01625) 545745
Website:
www.informationcommissioner.
gov.uk

Insolvency Service
Tel: 020-7291 6895
Website: www.insolvency.gov.uk

**Institute of Automotive Engineer
Assessors**
Stowe House
Netherstowe
Lichfield
Staffordshire WS13 6TJ
Tel: (01543) 266822
Fax: (01543) 266833
Website: www.iaea.uk.com

**Institute of Chartered Accountants in
England and Wales**
Chartered Accountants' Hall
PO Box 433
London EC2P 2BJ
Tel: 020-7920 8100
Fax: 020-7920 0547
Website: www.icaew.co.uk

**Institute of Chartered Accountants in
Ireland**
The Secretary
CA House
83 Pembroke Road
Dublin 4
Tel: (00 353 1) 637 7200
Fax: (00 353 1) 668 0842
Website: www.icai.ie

**Institute of Chartered Accountants of
Scotland**
CA House
21 Haymarket Yards
Edinburgh EH12 5BH
Tel: 0131-347 0280
Fax: 0131-347 0123
Website: www.icas.org.uk

Institute for Complementary Medicine
PO Box 194
London SE16 7QZ
Tel: 020-7237 5165
Website: www.i-c-m.org.uk

Institute of Plumbing and Heating Engineering
64 Station Lane
Hornchurch
Essex RM12 6NB
Tel: (01708) 472791
Fax: (01708) 448987
Website: www.plumbers.org.uk

Institute of Public Loss Assessors
14 Red Lion Street
Chesham
Buckinghamshire HP5 1HB
Tel: (01494) 782342
Fax: (01494) 774928
Website: www.mroffe.freeserve.co.uk/contactl.htm

Institute of Trichologists
24 Langroyd Road
London SW17 7PL
Tel: (08706) 070602
Website: www.trichologists.org.uk

Insurance Ombudsman Bureau (IOB)
See the Financial Ombudsman Service

International Air Transport Association (IATA)
2nd Floor
Central House
Lampton Road
Hounslow
Middlesex TW3 1HY
Tel 020-8607 6262
Fax: 020-8607 6350
Website: www1.iata.org

Investment Management Regulatory Organisation Ltd (IMRO)
Contact through the Financial Services Authority
Website: www.fsa.gov.uk

Joint Contracts Tribunal
9 Cavendish Place
London W1G 0QD
Tel: 020-7637 8650
Fax: 020-7637 8670
Website: www.jctltd.co.uk

Law Society of England and Wales
Law Society Hall
113 Chancery Lane
London WC2A 1PL
Tel: 020-7242 1222
Fax: 020-7831 0344
Website: www.lawsociety.org.uk

Law Society of Northern Ireland
Law Society House
98 Victoria Street
Belfast BT1 3JZ
Tel: 028-9023 1614
Fax: 028-9023 2606
Website: www.lawsoc-ni.org

Law Society of Scotland
26 Drumsheugh Gardens
Edinburgh EH3 7YR
Tel: 0131-226 7411
Fax: 0131-225 2934
Website: www.lawscot.org.uk

Lay Observer for Northern Ireland
4th Floor
Brookmount Buildings
42 Fountain Street
Belfast BT1 5EE
Tel: 028-9033 1857

Leasehold Advisory Service (LEASE)
4th Floor
70–74 City Road
London EC1Y 2BJ
Tel: 020-7490 9580
Fax: 020-7253 2043
Website: www.lease-advice.org

Legal Services Ombudsman
3rd Floor
Sunlight House
Quay Street
Manchester M3 3JZ
Tel: (0845) 601 0794
0161-839 7262
Fax: 0161-832 5446
Website: www.olso.org

Local Government Ombudsman
England
London boroughs north of the River
Thames (including Richmond but not
including Harrow or Tower Hamlets),
Buckinghamshire, Berkshire,
Hertfordshire, Essex, Kent, Surrey,
Suffolk, East Sussex, West Sussex and
Coventry City
Local Government Ombudsman
10th Floor, Millbank Tower
Millbank
London SW1P 4QP
Tel: 020-7217 4620
Fax: 020-7217 4621
Website: www.lgo.org.uk

London borough of Tower Hamlets,
Birmingham City, Solihull, Cheshire,
Derbyshire, Nottinghamshire,
Lincolnshire and the North of England
(except the Cities of York and Lancaster)
Local Government Ombudsman
Beverley House
17 Shipton Road
York YO30 5FZ
Tel: (01904) 380200
Fax: (01904) 380269
Website: www.lgo.org.uk

London boroughs south of the River
Thames (except Richmond) and Harrow;
the Cities of York and Lancaster and the
rest of England not included above
Local Government Ombudsman
The Oaks No 2
Westwood Way
Westwood Business Park
Coventry CV4 8JB
Tel: 024-7682 0000
Fax: 024-7682 0001
Website: www.lgo.org.uk

Scottish Public Services Ombudsman
4 Melville Place
Edinburgh EH3 7NS
Tel: (0870) 011 5378
Fax: (0870) 011 5379
Website:
www.scottishombudsman.org.uk

Local Government Ombudsman for
Wales
Derwen House
Court Road
Bridgend CF31 1BN
Tel: (01656) 661325
Fax: (01656) 673279
Website:
www.ombudsman-wales.org

London Transport Users Committee
(LTUC)
6 Middle Street
London EC1A 7JA
Tel: 020-7505 9000
Fax: 020-7505 9003
Website: www.ltuc.org.uk

Mail Order Protection Scheme
(MOPS)
3rd Floor
18a Kings Street
Maidenhead
Berkshire SL6 1EF
Tel: (01628) 641930
Fax: (01628) 637112
Website: www.mops.org.uk

Mailing Preference Service (MPS)
DMA House
70 Margaret Street
London W1W 8SS
Tel: 020-7291 3310
Fax: 020-7323 4226
Website: www.mpsonline.org.uk

Mediation UK
Alexander House
Telephone Avenue
Bristol BS1 4BS
Tel: 0117-904 6661
Fax: 0117-904 3331
Website: www.mediationuk.org.uk

Meteorological Office
FitzRoy Road
Exeter EX1 3PB
Tel: (0870) 900 0100
Fax: (0870) 900 5050
Website: www.metoffice.com

Motor Accident Solicitors' Society
54 Baldwin Street
Bristol BS1 1QW
Tel: 0117-929 2560
Fax: 0117-904 7220
Website: www.mass.org.uk

Motor Insurers' Bureau (MIB)
6–12 Capital Drive
Linford Wood House
Linford Wood
Milton Keynes MK14 6XT
Tel: (01908) 830001
Fax: (01908) 671681
Website: www.mib.org.uk

National Association of Estate Agents (NAEA)
Arbon House
21 Jury Street
Warwick CV34 4EH
Tel: (01926) 496800
Website: www.naea.co.uk

National Federation of Roofing Contractors
24 Weymouth Street
London W1G 7LX
Tel: 020-7436 0387
Website: www.nfrc.co.uk

National House Building Council (NHBC)
Buildmark House
Chiltern Avenue
Amersham
Buckinghamshire HP6 5AP
Tel: (01494) 735363
Website: www.nhbc.co.uk

National Inspection Council for Electrical Installation Contracting (NICEIC)
Vintage House
37 Albert Embankment
London SE1 7UJ
Tel: 020-7564 2323
Fax: 020-7564 2370
Website: www.niceic.org.uk

National Institute of Medical Herbalists (NIMH)
Elm House
54 Mary Arches Street
Exeter EX4 3BA
Tel: (01392) 426022
Fax: (01392) 498963
Website: www.nimh.org.uk

National Register of Property Preservation Specialists (NRPPS)
11 Greenland Road
Barnet EN5 2AL
Tel: (01253) 697176
Website: www.nrpps.co.uk

National Savings
Customer enquiries: (0845) 964 5000
Website: www.nationalsavings.co.uk

Newspaper Publishers' Association Ltd
34 Southwark Bridge Road
London SE1 9EU
Tel: 020-7928 6928
Fax: 020-7928 2067

Newspaper Society
Bloomsbury House
74–77 Great Russell Street
London WC1B 3DA
Tel: 020-7636 7014
Fax: 020-7631 5119
Website: www.newspapersoc.org.uk

NHS Direct
Tel: (0845) 4647
Scotland: (0845) 424 2424
Website: www.nhsdirect.nhs.uk

Northern Ireland Advisory Committee on Telecommunications (NIACT)
3rd Floor
Chamber of Commerce House
22 Great Victoria Street
Belfast BT2 7QA
Tel: (0845) 714 5000
Fax: 028-9024 7024
Website: www.ofcom.org.uk

Nursing & Midwifery Council
23 Portland Place
London W1B 1PZ
Tel: 020-7637 7181
Website: www.nmc-uk.org

Office of Communications (OFCOM)
Riverside House
2a Southwark Bridge Road
London SE1 9HA
Tel: (0845) 456 3000
Website: www.ofcom.org.uk

Office of Fair Trading (OFT)
Fleetbank House
2–6 Salisbury Square
London EC4Y 8JX
General enquiries: (0845) 722 4499
Website: www.oft.gov.uk

Office of Gas and Electricity Markets (OFGEM)
9 Millbank
London SW1P 3GE
Consumer helpline: (0845) 906 0708
Website: www.ofgem.gov.uk
         www.ofgas.gov.uk

Office of the Ombudsman for Estate Agents
Beckett House
4 Bridge Street
Salisbury SP1 2LX
Tel: (01722) 333306
Fax: (01722) 332296
Website: www.oea.co.uk

Office of Rail Regulation (ORR)
1 Waterhouse Square
138–142 Holborn
London EC1N 2TQ
Tel: 020-7282 2000
Fax: 020-7282 2040
Website: www.rail-reg.gov.uk

Office for the Regulation of Electricity and Gas (OFREG)
Website: http://ofreg.nics.gov.uk

Office of Telecommunications Ombudsman (OTELO)
PO Box 730
Warrington WA4 6WU
Tel: (0845) 050 1614
Fax: (0845) 050 1615
Website: www.otelo.org.uk

Office of Water Services (OFWAT)
Centre City Tower
7 Hill Street
Birmingham B5 4UA
Tel: 0121-625 1300
Fax: 0121-625 1400
Website: www.ofwat.gov.uk

Organisation for Timeshare in Europe (OTE)
Consumer Services Department
Rue Defaqz 78–80
Brussels 1060
Belgium
Fax: (00 32 2) 533 3061
Website: www.ote-info.com

Patients Association
PO Box 935
Harrow
Middlesex HA1 3YJ
Tel: 020-8423 9111
Fax: 020-8423 9119
Helpline: (0845) 608 4455
Website:
www.patients-association.com

Pensions Advisory Service (OPAS)
11 Belgrave Road
London SW1V 1RB
Tel: (0845) 601 2923
Fax: 020-7233 8016
Website: www.opas.org.uk

Pensions Ombudsman
11 Belgrave Road
London SW1V 1RB
Tel: 020-7834 9144
Fax: 020-7821 0065
Website:
www.pensions-ombudsman.org.uk

Personal Investment Authority
Contact through the Financial Services Authority

Personal Investment Authority Ombudsman
See Financial Ombudsman Service

The Postal Services Commission
Hercules House
Hercules Road
London SE1 7DB
Tel: 020-7593 2100
Fax: 020-7593 2142
Website: www.postcomm.gov.uk

Postwatch
Central Office
28 Grosvenor Gardens
London SW1W 0TT
Customer helpline: (0845) 601 3265
Fax: 020-7730 3394
Website: www.postwatch.co.uk

Radio, Electrical and Television Retailers' Association (RETRA)
Retra House
St John's Terrace
1 Ampthill Street
Bedford MK42 9EY
Tel: (01234) 269110
Fax: (01234) 269609
Website: www.retra.co.uk

Rail Passengers Council
Freepost WA1521
Warrington WA4 6GP
Tel: (0845) 302 2022
Fax: (0845) 850 1392
Website: www.railpassengers.org.uk

Registry of County Court Judgments
Registry Trust Ltd
173–175 Cleveland Street
London W1T 6QR
Tel: 020-7380 0133
Website: www.registry-trust.org.uk

Retail Motor Industry Federation
Consumer helpline: (0845) 758 5350
Website: www.rmif.co.uk

Royal Institute of British Architects (RIBA)
66 Portland Place
London W1B 1AD
Tel: 020-7580 5533
Fax: 020-7255 1541
Website: www.riba.org

Royal Institution of Chartered Surveyors (RICS)
Contact Centre
Surveyor Court
Westwood Way
Coventry CV4 8JE
Tel: (0870) 333 1600
Fax: 020-7334 3811
Website: www.rics.org.uk

Royal Society for the Prevention of Cruelty to Animals (RSPCA)
Wilberforce Way
Southwater
Horsham
West Sussex RH13 9RS
Tel: (0870) 333 5999
Fax: (0870) 753 0284
Website: www.rspca.org.uk

Scottish Advisory Committee on Telecommunications (SACOT)
28 Thistle Street
Edinburgh EH2 1EN
Tel: 0131-226 7275
Fax: 0131-226 4181
Website: www.ofcom.org.uk

Scottish Daily Newspaper Society/ Scottish Newspaper Publishers' Association/Scottish Print Employers' Federation
48 Palmerston Place
Edinburgh EH12 5DE
Tel: 0131-220 4353
Fax: 0131-220 4344
Website: www.snpa.org.uk

Scottish Legal Services Ombudsman
17 Waterloo Place
Edinburgh EH1 3DL
Tel: 0131-556 9123
Fax: 0131-556 9292
Website: www.slso.org.uk

Scottish Motor Trade Association
Palmerston House
10 The Loan
South Queensferry
EH30 9NS
Tel: 0131-331 5510
Website: www.smta.co.uk

Scottish Public Services Ombudsman
4 Melville Street
Edinburgh EH3 7NS
Tel: (0870) 011 5378
Fax: (0870) 011 5379
Website:
www.scottishombudsman.org.uk

Securities and Futures Authority
Contact through the Financial Services Authority

Society of Homeopaths
11 Brookfield
Duncan Close
Moulton Park
Northampton NN3 6WL
Tel: (0845) 450 6611
Fax: (0845) 456 6622
Website: www.homeopathy-soh.org

Strategic Rail Authority (SRA)
55 Victoria Street
London SW1H 0EU
Tel: 020-7654 6000
Fax: 020-7654 6010
Website: www.sra.gov.uk

**Textile Services Association
(TSA Ltd)**
7 Churchill Court
58 Station Road
North Harrow
Middlesex HA2 7SA
Tel: 020-8863 7755
Fax: 020-8861 2115
Website: www.tsa-uk.org

Timeshare Consumers' Association
Hodsock
Worksop
Nottinghamshire S81 0TF
Tel: (01909) 591100
Fax: (01909) 591338
Website: www.timeshare.org.uk

Transco
NQT House
Warwick Technology Park
Gallows Hill
Warwick CV34 6DA
Tel: (01926) 653000
Website: www.transco.uk.com

Trust UK Ltd
Website: www.trustuk.org.uk

**United Kingdom Central Council for
Nursing, Midwifery and Health
Visiting (UKCC)**
See the Nursing and Midwifery Council

**Water Industry Commissioner for
Scotland**
Ochil House
Springkerse Business Park
Stirling FK7 7XE
Tel: (01786) 430200
Fax: (01786) 462018
Website:
www.watercommissioner.co.uk

**Welsh Advisory Committee on
Telecommunications (WACT)**
4 The Science Park
Aberystwyth
Ceredigion SY23 3AH
Tel: (01970) 636413
Fax: (01970) 636414

Which?
2 Marylebone Road
London NW1 4DF
Tel: 020-7770 7000
Fax: 020-7770 7600
Website: www.which.co.uk

Which? Books
PO Box 44
Hertford X
SG14 1LH
Tel: (0800) 252100
Fax: (0800) 533053
Website: www.which.co.uk

Zurich Insurance
Stanhope Road
Portsmouth
Hants PO1 1DU
Tel: (0800) 056 1759
Website:
www.zurichinsurance.co.uk

Useful website addresses

Community Legal Service Direct
www.clsdirect.org.uk
Community Legal Service site providing
access to consumer help and advice online

Consumer Direct
www.consumerdirect.gov.uk
Government site giving updated
information about consumer law

Court Service
www.courtservice.gov.uk
County Court site which gives access to
standard court forms including claim form

Leasehold Advisory Service
www.lease-advice.org
Gives free help on leaseholders' rights

Money Claim Online
www.moneyclaim.gov.uk
Provides Claim Form N1 online, for
starting a county court claim

Index